AF316835

The Ultimate Guide to Starting and Growing a Successful Tutoring Business

Maurice C. Hill, LPC, MBA

Disclaimer:

This book is intended for informational purposes only, and should not be construed as legal, financial, or professional advice. The author and publisher make no representations or warranties with respect to the accuracy, completeness, or suitability of the information contained herein, and will not be liable for any damages, losses, or claims arising from the use of or reliance on the information provided in this book.

Readers are advised to consult with qualified professionals, such as attorneys, accountants, or financial advisors, for specific advice and guidance on legal, financial, or professional matters related to their freight brokerage business.

The information provided in this book is based on the authors' research, expertise, and experience, and may not reflect the latest industry trends, regulations, or practices. The authors and publisher do not endorse or promote any specific products, services, or companies mentioned in this book, and readers are advised to conduct their own due diligence before making any business decisions or investments.

By reading this book, readers agree to release and hold harmless the authors and publisher from any liability or claims arising from the use of or reliance on the information provided herein.

We hope that our collective expertise and insights have provided valuable guidance and support for readers of this book, and we welcome your feedback and suggestions for future editions.

Copyright © 2023

All Rights Reserved

Dedication

To Dr. Ann Marie Mitchell Ed.D,

This book is dedicated to you, an extraordinary educator and champion for students from all socio-economic backgrounds. Your lifelong commitment to empowering students through education has been a driving force behind our endeavor.

Your unwavering dedication to providing quality education to students from diverse backgrounds has been a constant source of inspiration for my team and me. Your passion for equal opportunities and your belief in the transformative power of education have shaped the lives of countless students and motivated us to share our knowledge.

Your invaluable insights and guidance have greatly influenced the content of this book, equipping aspiring tutoring business owners with the knowledge and understanding to support students from all walks of life. Your determination to bridge educational gaps and dismantle barriers has set an extraordinary example for all of us.

It is a privilege to have you as a mentor, and your wisdom and experience have played a significant role in shaping the vision of this book. I am deeply grateful for the opportunity to share your profound wisdom and dedication with a wider audience.

Thank you, Dr. Ann Marie Mitchell, for your unwavering commitment to empowering students from all socio-economic backgrounds and for being a guiding light in the field of education. This book stands as a testament to your profound impact and serves as a tribute to your exceptional contributions to inclusive education.

Acknowledgment

I would like to express my deepest gratitude to the contributors who have played a vital role in the creation of The Ultimate Guide to Starting and Growing a Successful Tutoring Business. Their expertise, knowledge, and valuable insights have significantly enriched the content of this book and provided invaluable guidance to aspiring educators turned entrepreneurs.

First and foremost, I would like to extend my heartfelt appreciation to Towanda Henderson at Towanda's Private Tutoring. Her passion for education, dedication to engaging with students, and commitment to sharing best practices have been instrumental in shaping the chapters of this book. Towanda's invaluable contributions have helped shed light on the importance of effective planning and leveraging the power of technology to reach and engage with potential clients. Her expertise and insights have enriched the content of this book, ensuring that aspiring tutoring business owners have access to valuable strategies and techniques. I am deeply grateful for Towanda's unwavering support and her commitment to excellence in the field of education. Her impact on the success of this book is immeasurable, and I am honored to have collaborated with such a remarkable educator.

I would also like to extend my sincere thanks to Nickola S.

Hill. Her expertise and insights into building brand awareness have been instrumental in highlighting the significance of establishing a strong and recognizable brand identity in the competitive landscape of the tutoring industry. Her expertise has provided invaluable guidance on how to effectively position and differentiate oneself to attract and retain clients through social media.

Furthermore, I extend my gratitude to Dr. Ann Marie Mitchell Ed.D for her valuable contributions. Her profound knowledge and insight into building a referral network have provided a wealth of information on how to foster strong relationships and partnerships within the education community. Her guidance has helped aspiring tutoring business owners establish a robust network of referrals, ultimately leading to the growth and success of their enterprises.

Lastly, I would like to express my sincere appreciation to all the individuals who have supported and encouraged me throughout the process of writing this book. Your unwavering support and belief in the importance of empowering educators as entrepreneurs have been a constant source of motivation.

To all the contributors and supporters, your dedication, expertise, and generosity are deeply appreciated. This book would not have been possible without your invaluable contributions. Thank you for sharing your knowledge and passion, and for being an integral part of The Ultimate Guide to Starting and Growing a Successful Tutoring Business.

With heartfelt gratitude,

Maurice C. Hill

CONTENTS

Preface

Welcome to The Ultimate Guide to Starting and Growing a Successful Tutoring Business. This book has been a labor of love, ignited by my deep passion for both education and business. Throughout my journey as an undergraduate student, double majoring in education and business, I found myself constantly seeking ways to bridge these two areas of interest. Little did I know that this curiosity would lead me on an extraordinary path.

Fueled by my profound love for education and an unwavering entrepreneurial spirit, I pursued a master's degree in business administration (MBA) to gain a solid foundation in the world of business. But my thirst for knowledge did not stop there. Recognizing the significance of integrating counseling principles into education and entrepreneurship, I embarked on further education, completing a graduate degree in counseling as a stepping stone toward my doctorate studies in counselor education and supervision.

As I ventured into my own entrepreneurial endeavors and later embraced the role of an adjunct college professor, I discovered a pressing need for educators and aspiring educators to possess a deeper understanding of the skills required to build and thrive in successful educational businesses.

It was this realization that sparked the concept for this book.

Drawing upon my years of hands-on business experience, the invaluable insights gained from my educational journey, and the integration of counseling principles, I set out to create a comprehensive guide that would empower educators to bridge the gap between their passion for teaching and the realm of entrepreneurship.

The Ultimate Guide to Starting and Growing a Successful Tutoring Business represents the culmination of my personal journey, fortified by extensive research and practical wisdom. It is my sincerest hope that this book will serve as a guiding light, inspiring educators who aspire to transform their love for teaching into flourishing tutoring enterprises.

Within these pages, you will discover a treasure trove of knowledge, strategies, and actionable steps to navigate the intricate landscape of the tutoring industry. From honing your niche and developing a compelling brand to acquiring clients, managing operations, and fostering long-term success, this guide encompasses every facet of building and expanding a tutoring business.

As you embark on this transformative journey, remember that you are not alone. The insights shared in this book are rooted in years of experience, extensive research, and a deep understanding of the unique challenges and opportunities within the education and business sectors. My aim is to empower you, the educator-turned-entrepreneur, to create a business that not only fuels your passion for teaching but also grants you the fulfillment and financial prosperity you deserve.

I invite you to delve into the chapters that lie ahead, armed with a thirst for knowledge and an unwavering commitment to your vision. Embrace the practical advice, learn from real-world examples, and adopt the strategies that resonate with your distinct tutoring business.

May this book become your trusted companion as you navigate the intricacies of launching and expanding your tutoring enterprise. May it ignite your inspiration, kindle your motivation, and equip you with the tools and insights necessary to realize your dreams. Remember, the impact you wield as an educator-turned-entrepreneur. You possess the power to shape the lives of countless students and leave an indelible legacy.

Here's to your resounding success as you embark on this remarkable journey!

Introduction

Starting a tutoring business can be an incredibly fulfilling and lucrative endeavor for those with a passion for education and helping others. As a tutor, you have the opportunity to make a difference in the lives of your students by helping them achieve their academic goals, building their confidence, and inspiring them to reach their full potential.

However, launching a successful tutoring business requires more than just a passion for teaching. In today's competitive marketplace, it's essential to have a deep understanding of the industry, as well as the business strategies and effective tutoring practices needed to thrive.

That's where The Ultimate Guide to Starting and Growing a Successful Tutoring Business comes in. This book provides a comprehensive roadmap for aspiring and existing tutoring business owners to build a thriving and sustainable enterprise.

We have written this guide with a goal to share our knowledge and experience to help you create a successful and profitable tutoring business. This book will cover everything from identifying your target market, developing your niche, setting up your business structure, creating a marketing strategy, and providing quality tutoring services.

With the insights and practical tips shared throughout this book, we aim to equip you with the necessary tools to navigate the various stages of your business journey successfully. Additionally, we have included real-world examples and insights from successful tutoring business owners to inspire and guide you along the way.

Whether you're just starting out or looking to grow and scale your existing tutoring business, The Ultimate Guide to Starting and Growing a Successful Tutoring Business has something for everyone. We believe that with the right knowledge, strategies, and passion, you can build a thriving tutoring business that will make a difference in the lives of your students and bring you financial success.

Chapter One

Why Start a Tutoring Business?

Starting a tutoring business can be an incredibly rewarding and lucrative endeavor for individuals with a passion for teaching and helping others. However, before diving into the details of starting a tutoring business, it's crucial to understand why you want to start one in the first place.

When it comes to starting a tutoring business, there are many reasons why people decide to pursue this venture. Some may have a love for teaching and want to share their knowledge with others. Others may be looking for a flexible work arrangement that allows them to balance other commitments, such as family or education. And, of course, the potential for earning extra income is also a significant motivator for many.

While these reasons may seem straightforward, it's crucial to take a deeper dive into your motivations and goals to ensure that starting a tutoring business aligns with your values and aspirations. For example, if you are passionate about teaching and want to make a difference in the lives of your students, you may need to consider whether the demands of running a business align with your goals. Similarly, if your primary motivation is to earn extra income, you may need to consider whether the tutoring market in your area is competitive enough to support your business.

Understanding your motivations and goals is essential to building a successful tutoring business. It will help you set realistic expectations, develop a business plan that aligns with your values, and stay motivated throughout the journey. By taking the time to reflect on your motivations and goals, you will be better equipped to make informed decisions and create a tutoring business that is both fulfilling and profitable.

For many people, a passion for teaching is the primary motivation for starting a tutoring business. As a tutor, you have the opportunity to make a significant impact on the lives of your students by providing personalized and effective instruction that helps them achieve their academic goals. Whether you are working with students who are struggling with a particular subject or helping high-achieving students reach even greater heights, tutoring allows you to share your knowledge and expertise in a way that can positively affect their lives.

In addition to academic achievement, tutoring can also help students build confidence and self-esteem. By providing students with individualized attention and guidance, you can help them overcome challenges and develop the skills and knowledge they need to succeed in school and beyond. This can be incredibly rewarding as you witness firsthand the growth and progress of your students.

Beyond personal fulfillment, tutoring can also be a way to make a difference in the world while pursuing your career aspirations. By helping students succeed academically, you are contributing to their future success and the betterment of society as a whole. This can be especially true for students who may not have access to traditional educational resources or who may be facing other challenges in their lives.

Ultimately, a passion for teaching is a powerful motivation for starting a tutoring business. It can be incredibly fulfilling to know that you are making a difference in the lives of your students and contributing to their future success. If you have a love for teaching and a desire to help others achieve their goals, tutoring may be the perfect career path for you.

Starting a tutoring business can offer the benefit of flexible working hours, which can be especially appealing for those who have other commitments, such as family or educational pursuits. As a tutor, you can typically set your own schedule and choose the hours that work best for you and your clients.

This level of flexibility allows tutors to pursue other interests or commitments while still earning income through their tutoring business. For example, if you have young children, you may choose to schedule tutoring sessions during school hours and then be available to spend time with your family in the afternoons and evenings. Alternatively, if you're pursuing an educational degree, you may choose to work as a tutor on a part-time basis to supplement your income while still allowing time for coursework and study.

The ability to work part-time or on a flexible schedule can also be beneficial for individuals who are transitioning into retirement. Tutors can continue to work and earn income while still having the flexibility to pursue other interests and hobbies.

Overall, the flexibility that comes with starting a tutoring business can be incredibly beneficial for those who have other commitments or interests. It allows for a better work-life balance, increased control over one's schedule, and the ability to pursue other passions and pursuits while still earning income.

The potential for earning extra income is one of the most significant factors driving people to consider starting a tutoring business. With the private tutoring industry projected to reach $227 billion globally by 2022, this field has significant potential for growth and profitability. Tutors can charge hourly rates that are often higher than the wages for traditional teaching jobs, and there is a high demand for quality tutoring services in many markets.

However, it's essential to note that building a successful tutoring business requires a significant investment of time, effort, and resources. Tutors need to invest time in building relationships with clients, marketing their services, and continuously improving their teaching skills. They may also need to invest in resources such as textbooks, learning materials, and technology to provide their students the best possible tutoring experience.

Additionally, the tutoring industry can be highly competitive, so it's crucial to have a solid understanding of the market, potential customers, and competitors. Success in the tutoring business requires an entrepreneurial spirit, business acumen, and a willingness to learn and adapt to changes in the market continuously.

While the ability to generate additional income is undoubtedly a significant motivation for many tutors, it's important to approach this opportunity with a realistic understanding of the investment required to build a successful tutoring business. With careful planning and execution, however, the potential for growth and profitability in the tutoring industry is significant.

Understanding your motivations and goals is critical to building a successful tutoring business. In the following sections of this book, we will explore the various motivations for starting a tutoring business, including a love for teaching, a desire for flexible working hours, and the capacity to generate additional income. We will also provide a framework for understanding your goals and aspirations, including identifying your educational background and teaching experience, determining the subjects or areas you are most passionate about, and defining your target clients and their specific needs.

By taking the time to reflect on your motivations and goals, you will be better equipped to make informed decisions and create a tutoring business that aligns with your values and aspirations. This will help you set realistic expectations, develop a business plan that aligns with your values, and stay motivated throughout the journey. Whether you are just starting out or looking to grow and scale your existing tutoring business, understanding your motivations and goals will be critical to your success.

Throughout this book, we will share practical tips, real-world examples, and insights from successful tutoring business owners to help you navigate the various stages of your business journey. We will cover everything from identifying your target market and developing your niche to setting up your business structure, creating a marketing strategy, and providing quality tutoring services. By following the guidance in this book and understanding your motivations and goals, you can build a tutoring business that is both fulfilling and profitable.

Starting a tutoring business can be a challenging but rewarding venture. As mentioned, it requires a significant investment of time, effort, and resources, making it crucial to approach this venture with a clear understanding of your motivations and goals. Evaluating your educational background and teaching experience is an essential first step, as this will help you identify your strengths and limitations as a tutor. It's also crucial to understand your target client's needs, as this will help you tailor your services to meet their specific requirements.

Furthermore, with many tutoring services available, it's essential to differentiate yourself from the competition. Developing a unique selling proposition will help you stand out in the market and attract clients. Finally, it's crucial to consider your long-term vision for your tutoring business, whether it's expanding into new markets or hiring additional tutors. Having a clear vision will help you set goals and make informed decisions as you grow your business.

By answering these critical questions and taking the time to develop a business plan that aligns with your values and aspirations, you can turn your dream of starting a tutoring business into a reality. The following chapters of this book will delve deeper into the practical strategies and steps you can take to build and grow a successful tutoring business. With careful planning and execution, starting a tutoring business can be a fulfilling and profitable career choice.

Chapter Two

Identifying Your Target Market

Starting a tutoring business can be an incredibly fulfilling and rewarding venture. Whether you're a passionate educator looking to make a difference in students' lives or an entrepreneur seeking to build a profitable enterprise, tutoring offers a flexible and lucrative opportunity. However, to build a successful tutoring business, it's essential to identify and understand your target market. By doing so, you can tailor your services to meet your client's specific needs and preferences, providing them with a personalized and effective tutoring experience.

In this chapter, we will explore the critical steps involved in identifying your target market. We'll discuss the factors to consider when selecting your niche, conducting market research, and targeting your ideal clients. By understanding your target market and developing targeted marketing strategies, you can build a thriving and sustainable tutoring business that meets your client's needs and sets you apart from the competition.

Identifying your target market is a critical step in building a successful tutoring business. It involves understanding the specific needs and preferences of your potential clients and tailoring your services accordingly. By doing so, you can provide a personalized and effective tutoring experience that meets the needs of your clients

The Ultimate Guide to Starting and Growing a Tutoring Business

and sets you apart from the competition.

To identify your target market, start by considering the subjects or areas you specialize in and the age groups you prefer to work with. Are you a math tutor who enjoys working with high school students, or do you specialize in language tutoring for adults? Identifying your niche will help you focus your marketing efforts and attract the right clients.

Once you have identified your niche, conduct market research to understand your potential client's needs and preferences. Consider factors such as their learning styles, academic goals, and budget. This information will help you develop tailored tutoring services that meet your client's specific requirements.

It's also essential to consider the geographic location of your target market. Are you willing to travel to clients' homes, or will you offer online tutoring services? Understanding the logistics of delivering your services will help you target clients in specific areas and provide them with a convenient and efficient tutoring experience.

By identifying your target market and tailoring your services to their needs, you can build a reputation as a trusted and effective tutor, attracting a loyal client base and setting yourself up for long-term success. The following chapters of this book will delve deeper into the practical strategies and steps you can take to identify and target your ideal clients, making your tutoring business a profitable and fulfilling venture.

Some factors to consider when identifying your target market include:

Age range:

When identifying your target market for your tutoring business, one crucial factor to consider is the age range of the students you will be tutoring. Some tutors prefer to focus on a specific age group, while others may work with a broad range of students.

One benefit of targeting a specific age range is that it allows you to tailor your tutoring services to the unique needs and learning styles of that age group. For example, elementary school students may benefit from more interactive and hands-on teaching methods, while high school students may require more focused and structured tutoring sessions. By specializing in a particular age group, you can become an expert in that area and provide a more effective tutoring experience.

On the other hand, limiting your target market to a specific age range may also limit your potential client base. If you only tutor high school students, for example, you may miss out on opportunities to work with elementary or middle school students who also need tutoring services.

It's important to weigh the potential benefits and disadvantages when considering the age range of your target market. Ultimately, it will depend on your personal preferences and expertise as a tutor.

Subject area:

Specializing in a particular subject area can be an effective way to establish yourself as an expert in your field and attract clients who are seeking specific subject tutoring. By specializing, you can focus your marketing efforts and tailor your services to meet the specific needs of your target audience.

One significant benefit of specializing in a subject area is that you can charge a premium rate for your services, especially if you have extensive knowledge and experience in that subject. This can lead to higher earnings potential and a more lucrative tutoring business.

However, the disadvantage of specializing in a particular subject is that it may limit your client base. While there may be a high demand for tutors in specific subject areas, such as math and science, there may be fewer clients seeking tutoring in more niche subjects. Additionally, if you specialize in one subject area, you may need to expand your services or target a wider range of clients to maintain a steady stream of business.

Another potential disadvantage of specializing in a subject

area is that it may limit your ability to diversify your services. If you choose to specialize in one subject, it may be challenging to expand your business to offer tutoring in other subject areas, which could limit your growth potential.

In summary, specializing in a particular subject area can be a profitable and effective way to establish yourself as an expert in your field and attract clients seeking specific subject tutoring. However, it may also limit your client base and growth potential and require you to diversify your services to maintain a steady stream of business.

Geographic location:

Targeting clients in a specific geographic location can have both benefits and disadvantages for a tutoring business. One benefit is that it allows you to focus your marketing efforts and become known as the go-to tutor in a particular area. This can help you establish a strong reputation and attract more clients through word-of-mouth referrals.

Additionally, targeting clients in a specific geographic location can help you save time and resources on travel expenses. By focusing on clients within a certain radius, you can reduce travel time between appointments, allowing you to take on more clients in a given day.

On the other hand, targeting clients in a specific geographic location can limit your potential client pool. If you only offer services in one particular area, you may miss out on potential clients who live outside of that area or who prefer online tutoring services. This can limit your growth potential and make it more difficult to scale your business.

Another disadvantage of targeting clients in a specific geographic location is that it can increase competition from other local tutors. If there are already established tutors in the area, differentiating yourself and attracting clients may be difficult.

Overall, targeting clients in a specific geographic location can be a viable strategy for some tutoring businesses, but it's important to weigh the potential benefits and disadvantages before making a decision.

Demographics:

When identifying your target market for a tutoring business, it's important to consider the demographics of your potential clients. This could include factors such as income level, academic achievement, or specific learning needs. Targeting a particular demographic group can help you tailor your services and marketing strategies to better meet their needs.

For example, targeting low-income families may involve offering affordable pricing options or working with local community organizations to reach those who may not have access to traditional tutoring services. Targeting high-achieving students, on the other hand, may involve offering more advanced or challenging coursework and developing programs that help them reach their full potential.

While targeting a specific demographic group can be beneficial in terms of tailoring your services and marketing efforts, there are also some potential drawbacks to consider. It may limit your potential client base and make expanding your business into other areas or demographics harder. Additionally, it's important to ensure that you are not discriminating against any particular group or violating any laws or ethical standards.

Overall, targeting a particular demographic group can be a useful strategy for building a successful tutoring business, but it's important to approach it with sensitivity and caution to ensure that you are providing equal opportunities for all potential clients.

Learning preferences:

When identifying your target market, it's essential to consider their learning preferences, such as whether they prefer one-on-one or group tutoring, in-person or online tutoring, or a combination of both.

One-on-one tutoring allows for a personalized approach to learning, where the tutor can cater to the specific needs and pace of the student. This method can be highly effective in improving student performance, as it provides targeted instruction and support. However, the downside is that it can be more expensive for clients, and tutors may have limited availability.

Group tutoring, on the other hand, is a more cost-effective option and can allow students to learn from and collaborate with their peers. It can also be a more social and engaging learning experience for students. However, group tutoring may not be suitable for all students, as some may prefer a more individualized approach to learning.

In-person tutoring allows for face-to-face interaction between the tutor and student, which can be beneficial for building trust and rapport. It also allows for hands-on learning and immediate feedback. However, the downside is that it can be limited by geography and scheduling availability.

Online tutoring has become increasingly popular in recent years, as it offers greater flexibility and convenience for both tutors and students. It allows for tutoring sessions to take place from anywhere with an internet connection, and sessions can be recorded for future reference. However, online tutoring may not be suitable for all students, as some may struggle with online learning or require more hands-on instruction.

Ultimately, the choice of learning preference will depend on your target market and the type of tutoring services you offer.

Consider the benefits and disadvantages of each method and tailor your services to meet your clients' specific needs and preferences.

In conclusion, identifying your target market is an essential step in building a successful tutoring business. By understanding your potential clients' needs and preferences, you can tailor your services to meet their unique requirements and provide them with a personalized and effective tutoring experience. In this chapter, we explored the critical factors to consider when identifying your target market, including age range, subject area, geographic location, demographics, and learning preferences. While each factor has its benefits and disadvantages, it's essential to weigh them carefully to make informed decisions that will help you build a thriving and sustainable tutoring business. In the following chapters of this book, we will delve deeper into the practical strategies and steps you can take to identify and target your ideal clients, making your tutoring business a profitable and fulfilling venture.

Chapter Three

Developing Your Tutoring Niche

As a tutor, it's not enough to be a generalist. To succeed in the competitive world of tutoring, you need to find your niche and excel in it. By developing a strong and unique tutoring niche, you can differentiate yourself from the competition and attract a loyal base of clients who value your expertise and services.

But how do you go about developing your tutoring niche? There are several ways to do it. One way is to specialize in a particular subject area, such as math, science, or language arts. By focusing on one subject area, you can become an expert in that field and provide your clients with a more effective tutoring experience.

Another way to develop your tutoring niche is to focus on a particular age range, such as elementary, middle, or high school students. Each age group has unique needs and learning styles, and by focusing on one age group, you can tailor your services to meet their specific requirements.

You could also offer specialized services, such as test preparation, college admissions counseling, or homework help. These services can be in high demand, and by providing them, you can differentiate yourself from other tutors who offer more general tutoring services.

Another option is to provide tutoring services to a specific demographic group, such as low-income families or students with learning disabilities. By focusing on a specific group, you can tailor your services to meet their specific needs and provide a more effective tutoring experience.

Finally, you could offer a unique approach or methodology, such as project-based learning or interactive online tutoring. These approaches can help you stand out from other tutors and provide a more engaging and effective learning experience for your clients.

In this chapter, we will explore each of these methods in more detail and provide practical tips and strategies for developing your tutoring niche. By the end of this chapter, you will have a better understanding of how to identify your niche and position yourself as an expert in your field. So let's get started and find your niche in the tutoring world!

One of the keys to success in the tutoring business is developing a niche that sets you apart from the competition. This involves identifying a specific area of expertise or specialization and positioning yourself as an expert in that area.

Some ways to develop your tutoring niche include:

Specializing in a particular subject area, such as math, science, or language arts, is one of the many ways of developing a niche.

One specific strategy for a tutoring business to specialize in a particular subject area is to develop a strong brand identity that emphasizes your expertise and passion for that subject. This can be achieved through various marketing strategies, such as creating a website showcasing your credentials and experience in the subject, developing promotional materials highlighting your specialized knowledge and skills, and building a social media presence that engages with potential clients and showcases your expertise.

Another way to specialize in a particular subject area is to offer customized tutoring services that cater to the unique needs and learning styles of your clients. For example, if you specialize in math tutoring, you could offer personalized lesson plans that target specific areas of difficulty for your clients, use interactive teaching tools and games to make the learning process more engaging and provide ongoing assessments and progress reports to help your clients track their improvement over time.

Networking within your local community and building relationships with schools and other educational organizations can also help you establish yourself as a go-to expert in your subject area. By attending local events, offering free workshops or seminars, and volunteering your time and expertise, you can build a strong reputation and attract new clients through word-of-mouth referrals.

Examples of how to specialize in a particular subject area could include offering advanced coursework for students seeking to excel in a particular subject, developing specialized tutoring services for students with learning disabilities or other unique needs, or offering test preparation services for standardized tests such as the SAT or ACT. Additionally, you could position yourself as an expert in a specific subject area by publishing articles or blog posts on educational websites or social media platforms, speaking at conferences or educational events, or collaborating with other educators in your field to develop innovative teaching strategies and materials.

Consider specializing in a particular subject area, such as math, science, or language arts

A specific strategy for a tutoring business specializing in a particular subject area could be to offer a comprehensive program that includes not only tutoring but also test preparation and college admissions counseling. For example, a math tutoring business could offer an SAT/ACT prep program that includes a math-specific curriculum and practice tests, as well as assistance with college application essays and financial aid forms.

Another strategy could be to partner with schools and educational organizations to offer after-school tutoring programs in your subject area. This can help you reach a wider audience and establish yourself as a trusted and reliable source of academic support.

To further differentiate yourself from the competition, you could develop a unique teaching methodology or approach that sets you apart. For example, a science tutor could offer project-based learning that incorporates hands-on experiments and real-world applications, while a language arts tutor could focus on developing critical thinking and analytical skills through literature analysis and creative writing exercises.

Utilizing technology can also be an effective strategy for a tutoring business specializing in a particular subject area. This could include offering online tutoring services, creating educational videos and resources, or developing interactive learning platforms incorporating gamification and other engaging elements.

Overall, to succeed in a tutoring business specializing in a particular subject area, it's important to offer a comprehensive and unique approach that meets the specific needs of your target audience. By developing a strong brand identity and establishing yourself as an expert in your field, you can attract a loyal client base and build a thriving and sustainable tutoring business.

Focusing on a particular age range can be an effective strategy for developing a niche in the tutoring business

Here are some specific strategies to consider:

1. Tailor your teaching style to the age group: Each age group has unique learning needs and preferences. Elementary school students, for example, may respond well to interactive and hands-on teaching methods, while high school students may require more structured and focused tutoring sessions. Adapting your teaching style to the age group can help you provide a more effective tutoring experience and establish yourself as an expert in that area.

2. Develop age-appropriate tutoring materials: Creating age-appropriate tutoring materials can help you engage with your target audience and provide them with the tools they need to succeed. For example, you might create interactive games and activities for younger students or develop more advanced coursework and practice exams for high school students.

3. Partner with schools and community organizations: Partnering with schools and community organizations can help you reach your target audience and establish yourself as a trusted resource in the community. Consider offering your services at local schools or community centers, or developing partnerships with organizations that serve the age group you are targeting.

4. Use social media to reach your target audience: Social media

platforms like Facebook, Instagram, and TikTok can be effective tools for reaching younger audiences. Consider developing social media content that speaks directly to the age group you are targeting, such as short educational videos or interactive quizzes and polls.

By focusing on a particular age range and tailoring your services to the specific needs of that group, you can establish yourself as an expert in that area and attract a loyal base of clients.

Offer specialized services, such as test preparation, college admissions counseling, or homework help

One specific strategy for a tutoring business that offers specialized services could be to create tailored packages for each service. For example, if you offer test preparation services, you could create different packages for the SAT, ACT, or other standardized tests. Each package could include a set number of tutoring sessions, study materials, and practice tests.

Similarly, if you offer college admissions counseling services, you could create packages that include services such as essay writing assistance, interview preparation, and application review. You could also offer add-on services, such as scholarship search assistance or financial aid advice, to further differentiate your business from competitors.

To promote these specialized services, you could create

targeted marketing campaigns that focus on your potential clients' specific needs and pain points. For example, for test preparation services, you could create social media ads or email campaigns highlighting the benefits of personalized tutoring and the success rates of your past clients. For college admissions counseling, you could create content such as blog posts or webinars that provide tips and insights on the college application process.

Overall, the key to successfully offering specialized services is to create packages and marketing strategies that meet the unique needs of your target audience and clearly differentiate your business from competitors.

Provide tutoring services to a specific demographic group, such as low-income families or students with learning disabilities

One specific strategy for providing tutoring services to a specific demographic group, such as low-income families or students with learning disabilities, is to partner with local schools and community organizations that serve these populations. This can help you reach a wider audience and establish yourself as a trusted and reliable resource for families and students in need.

Here are some steps to develop this strategy:

1. Identify local schools and community organizations that

serve low-income families or students with learning disabilities. This may include schools with high percentages of students receiving free or reduced-price meals or special education services, as well as organizations that provide services to families in need.

2. Reach out to these schools and organizations to introduce yourself and your tutoring services. Offer to provide free informational sessions or workshops to educate parents and students about the benefits of tutoring and your expertise in working with their specific demographic group.

3. Offer discounted rates or sliding-scale pricing to make your services more affordable and accessible for low-income families. Consider partnering with local businesses or organizations to provide scholarships or other financial assistance to families who may not be able to afford tutoring services.

4. Develop specialized tutoring programs that cater to the specific needs of students with learning disabilities, such as providing individualized learning plans, utilizing assistive technology, or partnering with other professionals such as speech therapists or occupational therapists.

5. Develop a strong referral network by partnering with other professionals and organizations that serve low-income families or students with learning disabilities, such as social

workers, psychologists, and special education advocates. This can help you reach a wider audience and establish yourself as a trusted and reliable resource in the community.

Offer a unique approach or methodology, such as project-based learning or interactive online tutoring

One specific strategy for a tutoring business specializing in a unique approach or methodology, such as project-based learning or interactive online tutoring, is to develop a strong online presence through social media and a company website. By showcasing your unique approach and methodology through online platforms, you can reach a wider audience and attract clients who are interested in innovative and engaging tutoring services.

To achieve this, consider the following steps:

1. Develop a strong brand identity that aligns with your unique approach or methodology. This can include creating a company logo, color scheme, and mission statement that reflect your tutoring services' values and goals.

2. Build a user-friendly and visually appealing website that showcases your tutoring services and unique approach. This should include a detailed description of your services, pricing information, testimonials from satisfied clients, and any relevant certifications or credentials.

3. Leverage social media platforms, such as Facebook, Twitter,

and Instagram, to promote your tutoring services and interact with potential clients. Consider sharing success stories, student testimonials, and informative content related to your unique approach or methodology.

4. Develop engaging and interactive online tutoring sessions that leverage technology and multimedia tools to enhance the learning experience. This can include using virtual whiteboards, interactive quizzes and games, and video conferencing software to create a personalized and dynamic tutoring experience.

5. Offer free trial sessions or discounts to attract new clients and encourage them to experience your unique approach or methodology firsthand. Consider partnering with local schools, libraries, and community organizations to offer workshops or informational sessions that showcase your tutoring services.

By developing a strong online presence and showcasing your unique approach or methodology, you can differentiate yourself from the competition and attract a loyal base of clients who value your innovative and engaging tutoring services.

In conclusion, developing a tutoring niche is essential for success in the competitive world of tutoring. By specializing in a particular subject area, focusing on a particular age range, offering specialized services, providing tutoring services to a specific demographic group, or offering a unique approach or methodology, you can differentiate yourself from other tutors and attract a loyal base of clients who value your expertise and services.

In the competitive tutoring business, it's important to develop a strong brand identity, tailor your services to meet the unique needs of your target audience and establish yourself as an expert in your field. Through targeted marketing campaigns, partnerships with local schools and community organizations, and a solid online presence, you can attract new clients and build a thriving and sustainable tutoring business.

So, whether you are a new tutor just starting out or an experienced educator looking to expand your services, finding your niche in the tutoring world is the key to success. So, go ahead and develop your niche, and let your expertise and passion shine through in your tutoring services!

Chapter Four

Setting Up Your Business Structure

As a tutor, your passion lies in helping students reach their full potential and achieve academic success. But to turn your passion into a successful business, you'll need to navigate the world of legal structures, registrations, and licenses. In Chapter 4 of this book, we will guide you through the process of setting up your tutoring business structure.

Choosing the right legal structure is an important step in setting up your tutoring business. It will determine the level of personal liability you'll have, the amount of taxes you'll pay, and the ease of raising funds or bringing on partners. We'll walk you through the most common business structures for tutoring businesses, including sole proprietorship, partnership, LLC, and corporation, so you can make an informed decision that meets your business needs.

Once you've chosen a legal structure, you'll need to register your business with your state and obtain any necessary licenses and permits. We'll provide you with a comprehensive checklist of the registrations and licenses you'll need, including business licenses, tax registrations, and professional licenses. We'll also explain the application process and provide tips for ensuring a smooth and successful registration.

By the end of this chapter, you'll have a clear understanding of how to set up your tutoring business structure, so you can focus on what you do best - helping students succeed. Let's dive in and get your business up and running!

Starting a tutoring business requires more than just identifying your target market and developing your tutoring niche. You also need to establish a solid legal and financial foundation to protect yourself and your business.

Choosing the right legal structure is an essential step in setting up your tutoring business. The four most common legal structures for small businesses include sole proprietorships, partnerships, limited liability companies (LLCs), and corporations. Each structure has its own benefits and drawbacks, depending on factors such as liability protection, tax implications, and management control.

The following are some of the most common business structures for tutoring businesses:

Sole proprietorship:

A business owned and operated by one person.

A sole proprietorship is a common business structure for many small business owners, including tutors. As a sole proprietor, you are the sole owner and operator of your business and have complete control over all aspects of your business operations. This structure offers many benefits, including ease of formation, minimal paperwork and legal requirements, and full control over business decisions and operations.

However, there are also drawbacks to operating as a sole proprietor. One of the most significant disadvantages is the lack of liability protection. As a sole proprietor, you are personally responsible for all debts and legal issues that arise from your business operations. This means that your personal assets, such as your home and savings, could be at risk if your business incurs any legal or financial liabilities.

Another potential disadvantage of operating as a sole proprietor is the tax implications. As a sole proprietor, you are taxed at the personal income tax rate, which can be higher than the tax rate for corporations or LLCs. Additionally, sole proprietors are not eligible for certain tax deductions and credits available to other business structures.

Finally, operating as a sole proprietor can also limit your ability to raise capital and expand your business. Without the ability to sell shares or take on partners, you may have difficulty accessing the funding you need to grow and scale your business.

In summary, while sole proprietorship offers many benefits, such as ease of formation and full control over business operations, it also has some drawbacks, including limited liability protection, potential tax implications, and limited access to capital. As a tutor, it's important to carefully consider these factors and weigh the pros and cons of sole proprietorship before choosing a business structure.

Partnership:

A business owned and operated by two or more people.

Partnerships can be an excellent business structure for those who want to share ownership and management responsibilities with one or more partners. There are several benefits to forming a partnership, such as sharing the workload, pooling resources, and taking advantage of different skill sets. In addition, partnerships often have more flexibility in terms of taxation and liability protection than sole proprietorships.

However, partnerships also come with their own set of drawbacks. One of the most significant risks of partnerships is the potential for personal liability. Unlike corporations or LLCs, partnerships do not provide any legal protection for the partners' personal assets in the event of business debts or legal issues. This means that each partner is personally responsible for the partnership's debts and liabilities.

Another potential downside to partnerships is the potential for disagreements or conflicts between partners. Since each partner has equal ownership and decision-making power, conflicts can arise if partners have different opinions on how the business should be run. It's essential to have a solid partnership agreement in place to address potential issues and outline each partner's responsibilities and decision-making authority.

Overall, partnerships can be an excellent choice for businesses that want to share ownership and management responsibilities. However, weighing the benefits and drawbacks is important, depending on factors such as liability protection, tax implications, and management control. Consulting with an attorney and accountant can help you make an informed decision about whether a partnership is the right structure for your business.

Limited liability company (LLC):

A hybrid business structure that combines the liability protection of a corporation with the tax benefits of a partnership.

One of the main benefits of an LLC is the limited liability protection it provides to its owners. This means that if the company incurs debts or faces legal action, the personal assets of the owners are generally protected.

Another benefit of an LLC is its flexibility in terms of management and ownership structure. LLCs can be managed by owners themselves, or they can hire a professional manager to oversee operations. In addition, LLCs can have an unlimited number of owners, which can be individuals or other businesses.

On the other hand, there are also some drawbacks to forming an LLC. One potential disadvantage is that the process of setting up an LLC can be more complex and expensive than forming a sole proprietorship or partnership. Additionally, LLC owners may be subject to self-employment taxes on their share of the company's profits.

Overall, whether an LLC is the right business structure for you will depend on factors such as the level of liability protection you need, the tax implications of the structure, and your desired level of management control. It's important to carefully consider these factors before making a decision on your business structure.

Corporation:

A legal entity that is separate from its owners and provides liability protection.

When it comes to setting up a corporation for your tutoring business, there are both advantages and disadvantages to consider. One of the primary benefits is that a corporation provides the greatest level of liability protection for its owners, also known as shareholders. This means that the personal assets of shareholders are generally protected from the company's liabilities, such as debts or lawsuits.

Additionally, corporations offer more flexibility in terms of ownership, management control, and structure. Shareholders can easily buy and sell shares of the company, and the board of directors can make important decisions about the business.

However, there are also some drawbacks to setting up a corporation. One of the most significant is the amount of paperwork and formalities required to establish and maintain a corporation. This includes filing articles of incorporation, adopting bylaws, holding annual meetings, and keeping detailed records.

In addition, corporations are subject to double taxation, meaning that the company's profits are taxed at the corporate level and again when distributed to shareholders as dividends. This can result in a higher overall tax burden for the company and its owners.

Ultimately, whether a corporation is the right choice for your tutoring business depends on various factors, such as the size of your business, the level of liability protection you need, and your tax goals. It's essential to carefully consider all of these factors and seek professional advice before making a decision.

In addition to choosing a legal structure, you'll also need to register your business with your state and obtain any necessary licenses and permits. This may include a business license, tax registration, and any required professional licenses.

Registering your business is an essential step in setting up your tutoring business. It not only ensures that your business is legal, but it also helps you to build credibility and establish a professional image.

The first thing you need to do when registering your business is to obtain a business license. The state or local government issues this permit, and it allows you to legally operate your business in the area. The requirements for a business license can vary depending on the state and locality, so it's important to research the specific requirements for your area. Some common requirements include completing an application, paying a fee, and providing proof of insurance.

Once you have obtained your business license, you'll also need to register your business for tax purposes. This involves obtaining a tax identification number, which is used to file your business's tax returns and pay any taxes owed to the government. You can obtain your tax identification number by registering your business with the Internal Revenue Service (IRS).

In some cases, you may also need to obtain a professional license in addition to your business license. This is especially true if you are providing tutoring services in a specialized area, such as special education or test preparation. The requirements for a professional license can vary by state and specialty, so be sure to check with your state's licensing board to determine the specific requirements in your area.

In conclusion, setting up a tutoring business can be an

exciting and rewarding venture. However, it's important to understand the legal and financial requirements involved in starting a business. Choosing the right legal structure, such as a sole proprietorship, partnership, LLC, or corporation, can impact your business's liability protection, tax implications, and management control. Once you've chosen a structure, registering your business with your state and obtaining necessary licenses and permits is crucial for legal operation and building credibility. By following the guidelines in this chapter, you'll be well on your way to establishing a successful tutoring business that helps students reach their full potential.

Chapter Five
Creating a Business Plan

As a tutor, you're passionate about helping students succeed. But to turn your passion into a successful business, you'll need a roadmap for success. That's where a business plan comes in.

A business plan is a critical tool for any tutoring business owner. It outlines your business goals, strategies, and financial projections and serves as a roadmap for building and growing your business. In this chapter, we'll guide you through the process of crafting a winning business plan for your tutoring business.

Business Plan

First, let's talk about why a business plan is essential. A well-crafted business plan can help you in several ways. A business plan is a critical tool that can help you clarify your business goals and strategies. When starting a tutoring business, it's important to have a clear vision of what you want to achieve and how you plan to get there. Without a solid plan, it's easy to get sidetracked and lose sight of your objectives.

One of the primary benefits of creating a business plan is that it forces you to think through all aspects of your business, from your target market and competition to your financial projections and marketing strategies. By outlining your goals and strategies in your business plan, you'll clearly understand what you want to achieve and how you plan to get there.

Your business plan should include a detailed description of your target market, including their demographics, needs, and preferences. This information will help you tailor your tutoring services to meet the specific needs of your target audience.

A business plan serves as a roadmap for your tutoring business, outlining the steps you need to take to achieve your goals. It provides a clear, organized path for your business and helps you stay on track and focused on your objectives.

By having a solid plan in place, you'll be able to anticipate potential roadblocks and challenges and develop strategies for overcoming them. A well-crafted business plan includes a timeline of milestones and goals, which can help you measure your progress and adjust your strategies accordingly.

Additionally, a business plan can help you communicate your vision and goals to potential investors, lenders, or partners. It provides a clear picture of your business, including your products or services, target market, financial projections, and marketing strategies. This information can be essential in securing funding, attracting investors, or developing partnerships that can help you grow and scale your business.

A well-crafted business plan is crucial if you're seeking to secure funding for your tutoring business. Whether you're looking to obtain a small business loan, attract investors, or even apply for grants, a comprehensive business plan can help you secure the funding you need to grow your business.

Investors and lenders want to see that you have a solid plan in place and that you understand the potential risks and rewards of your business. A business plan helps you demonstrate this by providing detailed information about your target market, competition, marketing strategies, financial projections, and more.

Your business plan will also outline how you plan to use the funding you receive. Whether you're looking to expand your business, purchase new equipment, or hire additional staff, your business plan will clearly explain how the funding will be used and how it will help you achieve your business goals.

In addition to securing funding, a business plan can also help you identify potential challenges and risks that could impact your business. By outlining potential roadblocks and developing contingency plans, you can prepare yourself for any obstacles that may arise and ensure your business stays on track.

A well-written business plan not only helps you clarify your business goals and strategies but also serves as a powerful tool for guiding your decision-making. By outlining the key components of your business, such as your target market, competition, and marketing strategies, a business plan can help you evaluate potential opportunities and risks.

For example, if you're considering expanding your services to a new market, a business plan can help you assess the feasibility of this expansion by analyzing factors such as market size, competition, and customer demand. By weighing the potential benefits and drawbacks of this decision, you can make an informed decision that aligns with your overall business goals and strategies.

Similarly, a business plan can also help you identify potential risks to your business and develop strategies to mitigate these risks. By anticipating potential challenges, such as changes in the market or increased competition, you can develop contingency plans and adjust your strategies as needed.

Now that you understand the importance of a business plan let's talk about how to create one for your tutoring business. Some key elements of a tutoring business plan include:

- Executive summary: A brief overview of your business and its goals.
- Market analysis: An analysis of your target market, competition, and industry trends.
- Services and products: A description of your tutoring services and any additional products or services you offer.
- Marketing and sales strategies: A plan for promoting and

selling your services to your target market.

- Financial projections: A detailed financial forecast that includes projected revenue, expenses, and profit.

Executive Summary

It is the opening section of a business plan and provides a brief overview of the entire document. This section should be concise yet informative, as it sets the tone for the rest of the plan and should entice the reader to continue reading.

The Executive Summary typically includes the following elements:

- Mission statement: This statement provides a brief overview of your tutoring business's purpose and guiding principles. It should be clear and concise and convey the essence of your business in a single sentence.

- Business goals: This section outlines the specific goals your business aims to achieve. These goals should be realistic, measurable, and aligned with your mission statement.

- Key strategies: This section outlines the key strategies your business will use to achieve its goals. This may include marketing and sales strategies, product or service development, or operational strategies.

The Executive Summary should be written last after you have completed the rest of the business plan. It should be a concise summary of the most important points in your plan and written in a compelling and persuasive way.

Some tips for writing a strong Executive Summary include:

- Keep it brief: The Executive Summary should be no more than two pages long.
- Use clear, concise language: Use simple language that is easy to understand and avoid technical jargon.
- Highlight your unique selling proposition: This is what sets your tutoring business apart from the competition. Make sure to highlight your unique selling proposition in the Executive Summary.
- Emphasize your financial projections: Investors will be interested in your financial projections, so make sure to include them in the Executive Summary.
- Proofread carefully: The Executive Summary is the first thing that investors and potential partners will read, so it's important to make sure it's error-free and well-written.

Market Analysis:

The market analysis section of a business plan is where you demonstrate your understanding of the tutoring industry and the market in which you operate. It should include a detailed analysis of the industry and market trends, as well as information about your target market demographics and your competitors.

To conduct a market analysis, you can start by researching the tutoring industry and gathering information on the latest trends and developments. This may include reviewing industry reports, news articles, and academic research.

Next, you should conduct a thorough analysis of your target market. This should include demographic information, such as age, gender, education level, and income, as well as psychographic information, such as interests, values, and attitudes. You should also consider factors such as the size of your target market and the potential demand for your tutoring services.

In addition to analyzing your target market, you should also conduct a competitive analysis to understand the strengths and weaknesses of your competitors. This may include researching their pricing strategies, marketing tactics, and service offerings. By understanding your competitors, you can identify areas where you can differentiate yourself and develop a competitive advantage.

Services and Products:

The Services and Products section of a business plan outlines the specific tutoring services and products that your business offers or plans to offer in the future. This section should provide a detailed description of each service or product, as well as any relevant information on pricing, delivery methods, and quality assurance measures.

When developing this section, it's important to be as specific and detailed as possible. For example, if you offer tutoring services in multiple subjects, you should list each subject and provide a brief description of the types of tutoring services offered for each subject. Additionally, you may want to include information on the qualifications and experience of your tutors, as well as any unique features or benefits that your services provide.

If your tutoring business also sells products, such as study materials or software, you should include a detailed description of each product, as well as any relevant pricing and delivery information. You may also want to provide information on how your products are developed and tested, as well as any guarantees or warranties that you offer.

Marketing and Sales

The Marketing and Sales section of a business plan outlines the strategies that will be used to promote tutoring services or products and generate revenue. The following are some of the key components of this section:

- Target market: This section describes the characteristics of the ideal customer for the tutoring services or products, including demographics such as age, gender, education level, and income. This information will help guide the development of marketing strategies that are tailored to the target audience.

- Marketing strategies: This section outlines the specific tactics that will be used to promote tutoring services or products to the target market. This may include advertising, social media marketing, search engine optimization, content marketing, or other strategies.

- Sales strategies: This section outlines how tutoring services or products will be sold to customers. This may include online sales, in-person sales, or a combination of both. It may also include information on pricing strategies, such as discounts or promotions, that will be used to attract and retain customers.

- Competitive analysis: This section analyzes the competition in the tutoring industry and identifies the strengths and weaknesses of competitors. This information can be used to develop marketing and sales strategies that differentiate the business from its competitors.

- Sales projections: This section outlines the expected sales for the business over a specific period of time, such as the next year or five years. This information is based on the marketing and sales strategies outlined in the business plan and the market analysis. It helps to demonstrate the potential revenue of the business and its growth potential over time.

Management and Organization:

The Management and Organization section of a business plan provides a detailed overview of the management structure and organization of the business. This section outlines the key personnel, their roles and responsibilities, and how they will contribute to the success of the business.

In this section, it's important to include information about the qualifications and experience of the key personnel, as well as their specific duties and responsibilities. This includes information about the CEO or owner of the business, as well as any other members of the management team, such as the chief financial officer, chief marketing officer, or operations manager

It's also important to outline the organizational structure of the business, including how decisions will be made and how tasks will be delegated. This may include information about the board of directors, advisory board, or other groups that will help guide the strategic direction of the business.

Additionally, this section may include information about any strategic partnerships or key suppliers that the business relies on, as well as any plans for future growth or expansion. Overall, the Management and Organization section provides investors and stakeholders with a clear understanding of the leadership and management structure of the business and how it will operate on a day-to-day basis.

Financial Projections:

The financial projections section of a business plan provides a detailed analysis of the financial performance and expectations of the business. This section includes three key financial statements: the income statement, the balance sheet, and the cash flow statement.

The income statement, also known as the profit and loss statement, provides a summary of the business's revenue and expenses over a specific period, such as a month or year. This statement is used to calculate the net income or loss of the business during the period.

The balance sheet provides a snapshot of the business's financial position at a specific point in time. It shows the business's assets, liabilities, and equity and is used to calculate the business's net worth.

The cash flow statement provides an overview of the cash inflows and outflows of the business during a specific period, such as a month or year. It shows the business's sources and uses of cash and is used to determine the business's ability to generate cash to meet its financial obligations.

In addition to these three financial statements, the financial projections section of a business plan may also include a break-even analysis, which calculates the point at which the business's revenue equals its expenses, and a sales forecast, which predicts the expected sales revenue for the business over a specific period.

The financial projections section is essential for potential investors, as it provides a clear understanding of the business's financial viability and potential for growth. It is important to ensure that the financial projections are realistic and based on accurate data and assumptions.

Funding requirement

The Funding Requirements section of a business plan is critical if you're seeking funding from investors or lenders. It should outline the funding you need, what the funds will be used for, and how you plan to repay them.

When describing your funding needs, you should be as specific as possible. Provide a detailed breakdown of how much money you need, including a timeline for when you need the funds and how you plan to use them. For example, you might need funding to purchase equipment or hire additional staff to meet the increased demand for your tutoring services.

It's also important to explain how you plan to use the funds. This can include a detailed breakdown of the costs associated with each item or activity, as well as any contingencies you've planned for unexpected expenses.

When discussing how you plan to repay the funds, you should be clear about your repayment strategy. This might include a timeline for when you plan to repay the funds, as well as the interest rate and any other terms of the loan. If you're seeking equity investment, you might describe your plan for generating profits and paying dividends to investors.

Appendix

The appendix is an optional section of a business plan that includes any additional information that may be relevant to the business or helpful in supporting the other sections of the plan. It can be used to provide more detailed information that may not fit in the other sections, such as resumes of key personnel, legal documents, marketing materials, and other relevant information.

Some examples of items that could be included in the appendix are:

- Product or service descriptions
- Customer research or surveys
- Competitive analysis
- Financial statements and projections
- Legal agreements or contracts
- Marketing materials such as brochures, flyers, or

advertisements

- Licenses and permits
- Relevant articles or research studies

Including an appendix can help to provide more detailed information for investors or lenders or simply help to organize and present information in a more comprehensive manner. It's important to ensure that all information included in the appendix is relevant and supports the other sections of the business plan.

Crafting a winning business plan for your tutoring business requires time, research, and attention to detail. But by creating a well-crafted business plan, you'll have a roadmap for success and a clear understanding of what it will take to achieve your goals.

Business Plan for General Tutoring Business

The following is a sample business plan for a general tutoring business:

<u>Executive Summary:</u>

Our tutoring business, named "Atlanta Tutoring Services," aims to provide high-quality tutoring services to K-12 students in Atlanta, Georgia. Our mission is to provide personalized, one-on-one tutoring sessions that help students achieve their academic goals and reach their full potential. Our key strategies include hiring experienced and qualified tutors, utilizing technology to enhance the learning experience, and building strong relationships with students and their families.

Market Analysis:

The tutoring industry in Atlanta is highly competitive, with many established tutoring businesses and private tutors operating in the area. However, there is a growing demand for high-quality tutoring services due to the increasing academic pressure on students and the desire of parents to provide their children with the best possible education. Our target market includes students in K-12 grades who are struggling in one or more academic subjects, as well as high-achieving students who are seeking additional academic support.

Services and Products:

Atlanta Tutoring Services offers one-on-one tutoring sessions in a variety of academic subjects, including math, science, English, and social studies. Our tutors are experienced and qualified, with backgrounds in education and related fields. We also offer specialized test prep services for standardized tests such as the SAT and ACT. In the future, we plan to expand our services to include group tutoring sessions and online tutoring.

Marketing and Sales:

Our marketing strategy includes targeted advertising

through social media platforms, online directories, and local publications. We will also leverage word-of-mouth referrals and offer promotions to attract new customers. Our sales strategy involves offering competitive pricing and flexible payment options, such as hourly rates or package deals.

Management and Organization:

Atlanta Tutoring Services is owned and operated by John Smith, who has over 10 years of experience in the education industry. The business will be managed by a team of experienced professionals, including a director of operations and a marketing manager. We will also hire a team of part-time and full-time tutors who are qualified and experienced in their respective subjects.

Financial Projections:

Our financial projections are based on conservative estimates of revenue and expenses. We anticipate generating $500,000 in revenue in our first year of operations, with a net profit margin of 10%. Our expenses will include salaries for staff and tutors, rent for our office space, marketing, and advertising costs, and technology expenses.

Funding Requirements:

We are seeking $100,000 in funding to cover our initial startup costs, including office rent, hiring staff and tutors, and marketing and advertising expenses. We plan to use these funds to launch our business and establish a strong presence in the local tutoring industry.

Appendix:

Our appendix includes resumes of key personnel, marketing materials, and legal documents, including our business license and insurance policies. We also have a detailed list of our tutoring services, including subject areas and pricing information.

Business Plan for A Special Education Tutoring Service

The following is a sample business plan for a special education tutoring service:

Executive Summary:

ABC Special Education Tutoring Services is a business that aims to provide specialized tutoring services to students with special needs. Our mission is to empower these students to achieve academic success and reach their full potential. To achieve this mission, we will offer tailored one-on-one tutoring services and personalized learning plans for each student.

Market Analysis:

The demand for specialized tutoring services for students with special needs is increasing, with a growing number of parents seeking assistance for their children. Several local competitors in the

Atlanta area offer tutoring services, but we differentiate ourselves by providing tailored one-on-one services and personalized learning plans.

Services and Products:

Our tutoring services will include academic support in reading, writing, math, and study skills, as well as specialized instruction in areas such as speech and language, occupational therapy, and behavior management. We will also offer diagnostic assessments to evaluate student needs and track progress.

Marketing and Sales:

We will use a variety of marketing strategies to promote our services, including social media advertising, online listings, and networking with local schools and parent groups. We will also offer free consultations and trial sessions to potential clients. Our sales strategy will focus on building long-term relationships with our clients and offering flexible payment plans to make our services accessible.

Management and Organization:

ABC Special Education Tutoring Services will be owned and operated by a team of experienced educators with backgrounds in special education and tutoring. Our team will include certified special education teachers, speech and language pathologists, occupational therapists, and behavior specialists.

Financial Projections:

We project a total startup cost of $50,000, which includes equipment, supplies, and marketing expenses. Our projected revenue for the first year is $150,000, with a net profit of $50,000. Our revenue will come from hourly tutoring rates and diagnostic assessments.

Funding Requirements:

We are seeking a loan of $30,000 to cover startup costs and initial operating expenses. We plan to repay the loan over a period of three years with interest.

Appendix:

Our appendix will include resumes of our team members, testimonials from previous clients, and legal documents such as our business license and liability insurance policy. We will also include sample lesson plans and progress reports to demonstrate our approach to specialized tutoring services.

Business Plan for A Test-Prep Tutoring Business

The following is a sample business plan for a Test-prep tutoring business

Executive Summary:

ABC Test Prep is a test preparation tutoring business based in New York City. Our mission is to provide high-quality and personalized test preparation services to students in the area. Our goal is to help students achieve their target scores and gain admission to their desired schools.

Market Analysis:

The test preparation industry has seen a significant increase in demand due to the growing competition in the education sector. With the rise of standardized tests and the increasing importance of test scores in college admissions, more and more students are seeking professional test preparation services. In New York City, there is a high demand for test preparation services, and the market is highly competitive. However, there is still room for growth and innovation, and ABC Test Prep aims to fill this gap by providing high-quality and personalized services.

Services and Products:

ABC Test Prep offers test preparation services for various standardized tests, including the SAT, ACT, GRE, GMAT, LSAT, MCAT, and more. We offer both individual and group tutoring services, and we customize our approach based on each student's learning style and needs. We also provide access to practice materials and resources to help students prepare for their tests.

Marketing and Sales:

Our marketing strategy involves targeted advertising through social media platforms, such as Instagram and Facebook, as well as local print publications. We also plan to partner with schools and educational organizations to offer our services to their students. Our sales strategy involves offering competitive pricing and packages to attract students, as well as providing excellent customer service to ensure high levels of customer satisfaction.

Management and Organization:

ABC Test Prep is owned and managed by John Doe, who has over 10 years of experience in the education sector. Our team of tutors consists of highly qualified and experienced educators who specialize in test preparation.

Financial Projections:

ABC Test Prep aims to generate revenue through individual and group tutoring services. We project revenue of $500,000 in the first year and a growth rate of 10% per year for the next five years. Our operating costs include rent, utilities, tutor salaries, and marketing expenses. We project a net profit of $100,000 in the first year, which is expected to increase to $200,000 by the fifth year.

Funding Requirements:

We plan to finance our business through personal savings and a small business loan of $50,000. The loan will be used to cover start-up costs, including rent, marketing expenses, and purchasing equipment and materials.

Appendix:

Our appendix includes resumes of our key personnel, marketing materials, and legal documents, such as our business license and liability insurance. We also include our tutoring packages and pricing details for reference.

In conclusion, a well-crafted business plan is essential for the success of any tutoring business. It provides a roadmap for building and growing your business and serves as a valuable tool for securing funding and guiding your decision-making. By including key sections such as the executive summary, market analysis, services and products, marketing and sales, management and organization, financial projections, funding requirements, and appendix, you can ensure that your business plan is comprehensive and effective. Remember to continually review and update your plan to adapt to changes in the market and ensure that you are on track to achieving your goals. With a solid business plan in place, you can confidently move forward in building a thriving tutoring business.

Chapter Six

Developing a Marketing Strategy

As a tutoring business owner, you understand the importance of providing high-quality services to your clients. However, without a solid marketing strategy, reaching your target market and growing your business can be difficult. In Chapter 6, we will explore the various components of a successful marketing strategy for tutoring businesses. From developing a professional website to establishing referral partnerships, we'll cover a range of effective tactics that can help you connect with potential clients and stand out in a competitive market. Whether you're just starting out or looking to expand your client base, this chapter will provide you with the tools and insights you need to develop a marketing strategy that drives results. Get ready to take your tutoring business to the next level!

As a tutoring business owner, you understand the value of education and the impact it can have on your clients' lives. However, without a strong marketing strategy in place, it can be difficult to reach potential clients and communicate the value of your services.

One of the first steps in developing a marketing strategy is identifying your target market. Who are your ideal clients? What are their needs and pain points? Understanding your target market will allow you to tailor your marketing efforts to their specific needs and preferences.

Once you have identified your target market, you can begin to develop a marketing plan that includes a mix of online and offline tactics. Online marketing tactics may include developing a professional website that showcases your services and expertise, utilizing social media platforms to connect with potential clients and promote your services, and utilizing paid advertising on platforms such as Google AdWords or Facebook Ads.

Offline marketing tactics may include creating and distributing marketing materials such as brochures, flyers, and business cards to local schools, libraries, and community centers. Additionally, offering free trial sessions or discounted rates to new clients can be an effective way to encourage them to try your services and build a relationship with your business.

Another important aspect of developing a marketing strategy is regularly evaluating its effectiveness and making adjustments as needed. This may involve tracking metrics such as website traffic, conversion rates, and client feedback and using this information to make informed decisions about where to allocate your marketing resources.

By developing a comprehensive marketing strategy that effectively communicates your services and value proposition to your target market, you can attract new clients, build strong relationships with existing clients, and establish your business as a trusted and reputable provider of tutoring services.

Some effective marketing strategies for tutoring businesses include:

Developing a professional website that showcases your services and expertise

Developing a professional website is essential for any tutoring business looking to establish a strong online presence and attract potential clients. A well-designed website can showcase your services and expertise, provide valuable information to prospective clients, and ultimately lead to increased business and revenue.

When developing your website, it's important to keep in mind the needs and preferences of your target audience. Your website should be easy to navigate, visually appealing, and provide clear and concise information about your tutoring services. It's also important to ensure that your website is optimized for search engines, as this will improve your visibility in search results and help potential clients find your business.

In addition to showcasing your services and expertise, your website can also serve as a platform for communicating with clients and potential clients. This may include providing online scheduling and booking options, offering online resources and study materials, and allowing clients to leave reviews and feedback.

Ultimately, developing a professional website is an important component of any successful tutoring business. By investing in a well-designed website and regularly updating and optimizing it, you can attract and retain clients, establish a strong online presence, and grow your business.

Utilizing social media platforms, such as Facebook, Instagram, and Twitter, to connect with potential clients and promote your services.

Social media platforms have become an essential part of modern-day marketing, and they can be an effective tool for promoting tutoring services. By utilizing social media platforms such as Facebook, Instagram, and Twitter, tutoring businesses can connect with potential clients and promote their services in a cost-effective and efficient way.

Facebook is one of the most widely used social media platforms, with over 2 billion monthly active users. It offers a range of features that can be used to promote a tutoring business, such as creating a business page, running targeted ads, and joining relevant groups. A business page allows tutoring businesses to showcase their services and share valuable content with potential clients. Running targeted ads can help reach specific audiences based on demographics, interests, and behaviors. Joining relevant groups can also help to connect with potential clients and establish relationships with other professionals in the industry.

Instagram is another popular social media platform that can be used to promote tutoring services. It is a highly visual platform, and tutoring businesses can use it to showcase their services and share engaging content. Hashtags are an effective way to reach a wider audience on Instagram, and businesses can use them to target specific topics and interests. Instagram also offers features such as Instagram Stories and Instagram Live, which can be used to provide valuable information and engage with potential clients in real time.

Twitter is a fast-paced social media platform that shares short, snappy messages about tutoring services. It is a useful platform for sharing news and updates and engaging with potential clients and other professionals in the industry. Hashtags are also important on Twitter, as they can help to reach a wider audience and increase visibility.

In conclusion, social media platforms such as Facebook, Instagram, and Twitter can be powerful tools for promoting tutoring services. By utilizing these platforms effectively, tutoring businesses can connect with potential clients, establish their brands, and ultimately grow their business.

Creating and distributing marketing materials, such as brochures, flyers, and business cards, to local schools, libraries, and community centers

Creating and distributing marketing materials can be an effective way to increase awareness of your tutoring business and attract potential clients. Brochures, flyers, and business cards are all tangible marketing materials that can be distributed to local schools, libraries, and community centers

When creating marketing materials, it's important to ensure that they are visually appealing and provide key information about your business, such as your services, pricing, and contact information. Consider including testimonials from satisfied clients to help build credibility and trust.

Once your marketing materials are created, it's important to distribute them strategically. Identify local schools, libraries, and community centers that may be interested in your services, and make sure to leave your materials in visible and accessible areas. You can also attend local community events and distribute your materials to potential clients in person.

Remember to regularly evaluate the effectiveness of your marketing materials and adjust your strategy as needed. Creating and distributing high-quality marketing materials can increase awareness of your tutoring business and attract new clients.

Offering free trial sessions or discounted rates to new clients to encourage them to try your services

Offering free trial sessions or discounted rates to new clients is a powerful marketing tactic for tutoring businesses. By providing potential clients with a risk-free opportunity to experience your services, you can help build trust and establish your credibility as a reliable and effective tutor.

One effective approach is to offer a free initial consultation or assessment, which can help you better understand your client's needs and tailor your services to their specific goals. This can be a valuable tool in building a long-term relationship with your clients and increasing their satisfaction with your services.

Discounted rates can also be an effective way to encourage new clients to try your services. By offering a limited-time discount, you can create a sense of urgency and motivate potential clients to take action and sign up for your services.

It's important to ensure that any free trial or discount offers align with your overall business goals and financial projections. By carefully evaluating the costs and benefits of these offers, you can ensure that they are a sustainable and effective marketing strategy for your tutoring business.

Establishing referral partnerships with other professionals, such as teachers, counselors, and educational consultants

Establishing referral partnerships with other professionals in the education industry can be a valuable tool in expanding your tutoring business. By collaborating with teachers, counselors, and educational consultants, you can tap into their networks and gain access to potential clients who may be seeking additional support outside of the classroom.

To establish referral partnerships, you should begin by identifying professionals in your area who work with students in your target market. Reach out to them and introduce yourself and your services, highlighting the benefits of working together. You may want to offer a special discount or incentive for referrals to encourage them to refer clients to you.

Maintaining strong relationships with your referral partners is important to providing high-quality services and excellent customer service. Regularly communicate with them to update them on your services and any changes in your business.

By establishing referral partnerships, you can not only increase your client base but also build a strong reputation in the education industry and position yourself as a trusted resource for students and families.

In conclusion, developing a marketing strategy is crucial to any successful tutoring business. By identifying your target market, developing a professional website, utilizing social media platforms, creating and distributing marketing materials, offering free trial sessions or discounted rates, and establishing referral partnerships, you can attract potential clients and communicate the value of your services. Regularly evaluating and adjusting your marketing strategy based on metrics such as website traffic, conversion rates, and client feedback can also help ensure its effectiveness. By implementing these tactics and constantly striving to improve, you can take your tutoring business to the next level and establish yourself as a trusted and reputable provider of tutoring services.

Chapter Seven

Establishing Your Online Presence

Welcome to Chapter 7 of our tutoring business book, where we'll discuss the importance of establishing a strong online presence for your business. In today's digital age, the majority of consumers turn to the internet to research and connect with businesses, and tutoring businesses are no exception. By establishing a professional website, developing a social media presence, and utilizing online platforms to promote your services, you can increase your visibility, attract potential clients, and ultimately grow your business. In this chapter, we'll explore the various components of a strong online presence for tutoring businesses and provide you with the tools and insights you need to develop an effective online strategy that drives results. So let's dive in and explore the world of online marketing for tutoring businesses!

As a tutoring business owner, establishing a strong online presence is essential in today's digital age. It not only helps you reach a wider audience but also enables you to showcase your expertise and connect with potential clients. In this section, we'll explore some valuable tips for establishing your online presence, including strategies for developing a professional website, creating a social media presence, and effectively promoting your services on online platforms. Read on to discover how you can take your tutoring business to the next level with a strong online presence.

Developing a professional website that showcases your services and expertise

Developing a professional website is a crucial step for any tutoring business looking to establish a strong online presence and attract potential clients. A website can serve as a platform for showcasing your services and expertise, communicating with clients, and ultimately driving business and revenue.

The benefits of having a professional website are numerous. First and foremost, a well-designed website can help build credibility and trust with potential clients, who are increasingly turning to the internet to find tutoring services. A website can also provide valuable information to prospective clients, such as pricing, scheduling, and testimonials from satisfied customers. Additionally, a website can help improve your visibility in search results, making it easier for potential clients to find your business.

When developing your website, it's important to keep the needs and preferences of your target audience in mind. Your website should be visually appealing, easy to navigate, and provide clear and concise information about your tutoring services. It's also important to ensure that your website is optimized for search engines, as this will improve your visibility in search results and help potential clients find your business.

To develop a professional website, you may want to consider working with a web designer or using a website builder platform such as Wix or Squarespace. It's important to choose a design that is consistent with your brand and appeals to your target audience.

Here are 10 credible resources for building a website for a tutoring business:

- Wix - A website builder that offers a drag-and-drop interface and a range of templates for creating a website for your tutoring business.

- Squarespace - Another website builder that offers a sleek and modern design and various customization options to create an online presence for your tutoring business.

- WordPress - A popular platform that allows for easy customization and scalability for creating a website for your tutoring business.

- Weebly - A user-friendly website builder that offers a drag-and-drop interface for easily creating a website.

- GoDaddy - A website builder and hosting provider that offers a range of templates and features for creating a professional website for your tutoring business.

- Shopify - A platform designed for e-commerce businesses that offer a range of features to create an online store for tutoring products or services.

- Jimdo - A website builder that offers a range of templates and tools for creating a website for your tutoring business.

- Webs - A website builder that offers a drag-and-drop interface and various templates to create a website for your tutoring business.

- Webflow - A website builder that allows for advanced customization and design options to create a website for your tutoring business.

- SiteBuilder - A website builder that offers a range of templates and features to create a website for your tutoring business with no coding required.

Each of these resources offers various features and pricing options, so it's important to research and compare them to find the best fit for your tutoring business's specific needs and budget. Additionally, many online tutorials and resources are available to help guide you through the website-building process, such as the online help centers provided by each of the above resources, YouTube tutorials, and online courses.

In addition to showcasing your services and expertise, your website can also serve as a platform for communicating with clients and potential clients. This may include providing online scheduling and booking options, offering online resources and study materials, and allowing clients to leave reviews and feedback.

In conclusion, developing a professional website is an essential component of any successful tutoring business. Investing in a well-designed website and regularly updating and optimizing it can attract and retain clients, establish a strong online presence, and grow your business.

Creating a blog or resource center that offers valuable educational content for your target market

Creating a blog or resource center effectively showcases your expertise, provides valuable information to your target market, and establishes your tutoring business as a trusted resource in the education industry. Regularly publishing high-quality educational content can build a loyal following and increase your visibility online.

Creating a blog or resource center can benefit your tutoring business in several ways. First, it can help establish your business as a thought leader in the industry, increasing your credibility and attracting potential clients. Second, it can provide a platform for sharing valuable information and resources with your target market, which can help build trust and establish long-term relationships with clients. Finally, it can improve your search engine visibility, as regularly updated content can help improve your website's ranking in search results.

When creating a blog or resource center, it's important to

consider your target market's needs and preferences. What types of content are they looking for? What questions do they have? By understanding your target market's needs, you can tailor your content to their specific interests and provide value that will keep them coming back for more.

Your blog or resource center should also reflect your brand and the unique value proposition of your tutoring business. Consider including content that showcases your expertise, such as study tips, educational resources, and success stories from satisfied clients.

To maximize the effectiveness of your blog or resource center, it's important to publish content on a regular basis. This can help build a loyal following and improve your search engine visibility. Consider creating a content calendar and publishing schedule to ensure that you consistently provide value to your target market.

In addition to written content, you may also want to include other types of content, such as videos, infographics, or podcasts. This can help keep your content fresh and engaging and appeal to a wider range of learning styles.

Here are 10 platforms that can be used to create and manage a blog or resource center:

1. WordPress - A popular blogging platform offering various customization options and plugins for creating educational

content.

2. Squarespace - A website builder that offers a user-friendly interface for creating a blog or resource center.

3. HubSpot - A marketing and sales platform that offers a content management system for creating and publishing educational content.

4. Wix - A website builder offering various templates and tools for creating educational content.

5. Medium - A popular blogging platform that allows users to publish educational content and reach a wide audience.

6. Ghost - A platform designed specifically for blogging and content creation, offering a range of features for creating educational content.

7. Joomla - A content management system offering various customization options for creating a blog or resource center.

8. Drupal - Another content management system that offers a range of features for creating and publishing educational content.

9. Weebly - A website builder that offers a drag-and-drop interface for creating educational content.

10. Google Sites - A free website builder that allows users to create a simple blog or resource center with minimal setup required.

Overall, creating a blog or resource center is an effective

way to showcase your expertise, provide valuable information to your target market, and establish your tutoring business as a trusted resource in the education industry. By consistently publishing high-quality content and engaging with your target market, you can attract new clients, build strong relationships with existing clients, and grow your business.

Utilizing social media platforms, such as Facebook, Instagram, and Twitter, to connect with potential clients and promote your services

Social media platforms have revolutionized the way businesses connect with potential clients and promote their services. With billions of users on platforms such as Facebook, Instagram, and Twitter, social media has become a powerful tool for businesses of all sizes and industries to reach their target audience and build their brands.

For tutoring businesses, social media can be an effective way to connect with potential clients and promote their services in a cost-effective and efficient way. Social media platforms allow tutoring businesses to showcase their services, share valuable content, and engage with potential clients in real time.

One of the key benefits of social media is the ability to target specific audiences based on demographics, interests, and behaviors. This allows tutoring businesses to reach potential clients who are most likely to be interested in their services, increasing the effectiveness of their marketing efforts.

Additionally, social media platforms provide an opportunity for tutoring businesses to establish their brand and build a strong online presence. By regularly posting valuable content and engaging with their audience, tutoring businesses can establish themselves as trusted and reputable provider of tutoring services.

To utilize social media effectively, tutoring businesses should first identify their target audience and select the platforms that are most relevant to their audience. Facebook, Instagram, and Twitter are all popular platforms that can be effective for tutoring businesses, but the specific platform(s) chosen will depend on the target audience and the type of content being shared.

The following are some of the social media platforms that can be used for a tutoring business:

1. Facebook is a social media platform that allows users to connect with friends and family, share content, and join groups. Why: Facebook can be a powerful tool for promoting tutoring services by creating a business page, running targeted ads, and joining relevant groups. How: By utilizing Facebook's features effectively, tutoring businesses can connect with potential clients, establish their brand, and ultimately grow their business.

2. Instagram is a highly visual social media platform that allows users to share photos and videos. Why: Instagram can be used to showcase tutoring services and share engaging content. Hashtags can be used to reach a wider audience, and features such as Instagram Stories and Instagram Live can be used to engage with potential clients in real time. How: By creating a visually appealing profile and consistently sharing high-quality content, tutoring businesses can attract potential clients and establish their brand on Instagram.

3. Twitter is a fast-paced social media platform that allows users to share short messages. Why: Twitter is useful for sharing news and updates, as well as engaging with potential clients and other professionals in the industry. Hashtags can help to increase visibility and reach a wider audience. How: By regularly sharing updates and engaging with relevant hashtags and conversations, tutoring businesses can establish their presence on Twitter and connect with potential clients.

4. LinkedIn is a professional networking platform that allows users to connect with other professionals and showcase their expertise. Why: LinkedIn can be used to connect with other professionals in the education industry and establish referral partnerships. It can also be used to showcase tutoring services and share valuable content with potential clients.

How: By creating a professional profile, joining relevant groups, and sharing high-quality content, tutoring businesses can establish themselves as experts in the industry and attract potential clients.

5. TikTok is a social media platform that allows users to create and share short videos. Why: TikTok can be used to create engaging and educational content that appeals to younger audiences. It can also be used to showcase tutoring services creatively and entertainingly. How: By creating short, educational videos that showcase tutoring services and engaging with relevant hashtags and trends, tutoring businesses can reach a younger audience on TikTok.

6. Pinterest is a visual search engine that allows users to discover and save ideas. Why: Pinterest can be used to share educational resources and showcase tutoring services in a visually appealing way. It can also be used to drive traffic to a tutoring business's website. How: By creating boards that showcase educational resources and services and sharing high-quality images and content, tutoring businesses can attract potential clients and establish themselves as experts in the industry.

7. YouTube is a video-sharing platform that allows users to upload and share videos. Why: YouTube can be used to create educational videos that showcase tutoring services

and provide value to potential clients. It can also be used to establish a tutoring business as an expert in the industry. How: By creating educational and informative videos that showcase tutoring services, answering frequently asked questions, and engaging with comments and feedback, tutoring businesses can attract potential clients and establish themselves as experts in the industry.

8. Snapchat is a social media platform that allows users to share photos and videos that disappear after a short time. Why: Snapchat can be used to showcase tutoring services in a creative and engaging way. It can also be used to connect with younger audiences who may be seeking additional support outside of the classroom. How: By creating short, educational videos and sharing them with a relevant audience on Snapchat, tutoring businesses can attract potential clients and establish themselves as experts in the industry.

9. Reddit is a social media platform that allows users to post and engage with content in communities or "subreddits." Why: Reddit can be used to engage with potential clients and establish a tutoring business.

10. Quora is a question-and-answer website where users can ask and answer questions on a wide range of topics. It has a large and active user base, making it an ideal platform for

promoting tutoring services and establishing thought leadership in the education industry.

Each of these social media platforms has its own unique features and user base. Depending on your target market and business goals, you may want to focus your efforts on one or a few specific platforms. For example, Facebook is a popular platform for businesses to connect with potential clients and share information about their services, while Instagram is a highly visual platform that can be effective for showcasing your tutoring services and engaging with potential clients.

Once the platforms have been selected, tutoring businesses should develop a content strategy, including the right balance of promotional and educational content. Promotional content may include information about services, special offers, and client testimonials, while educational content may include study tips, helpful resources, and industry news.

It's also important for tutoring businesses to engage with their audience on social media by responding to comments and messages, sharing and commenting on relevant content, and participating in online conversations. This can help to build relationships with potential clients and establish the business as a knowledgeable and trustworthy source of information.

Ultimately, utilizing social media platforms such as

Facebook, Instagram, and Twitter can be a powerful tool for tutoring businesses to connect with potential clients, establish their brand, and ultimately grow their business. By developing a strong social media presence and regularly engaging with their audience, tutoring businesses can build a loyal client base and establish themselves as a leader in the industry.

Offering online tutoring services using video conferencing software, such as Zoom or Skype

In today's digital age, offering online tutoring services is becoming increasingly popular among students and parents. With the ability to connect with tutors from anywhere in the world, students can receive high-quality tutoring services from the comfort of their own homes. Video conferencing software, such as Zoom or Skype, allows tutors to communicate with students in real time and provide personalized support and guidance.

To offer online tutoring services using video conferencing software, tutors will need a reliable internet connection, a computer or mobile device with a webcam and microphone, and a subscription to a video conferencing software platform, such as Zoom or Skype.

Once the necessary equipment and software are in place, tutors can begin advertising their online tutoring services to potential clients. This may include creating a professional website or social media presence that showcases their services and expertise, offering free trial sessions or discounted rates to new clients, and establishing referral partnerships with other professionals in the education industry.

When conducting online tutoring sessions, it's important for tutors to create a structured and engaging learning environment. This may include utilizing interactive online tools, such as virtual whiteboards and screen sharing, to help students better understand complex concepts and engage with the material.

Tutors should also ensure that they have a clear understanding of their student's learning goals and needs and tailor their tutoring sessions accordingly. Regular communication with students and their parents can help to build trust and establish a strong relationship, which can ultimately lead to increased satisfaction with the tutoring services and referrals to new clients.

The following are ten tools that can be used for offering online tutoring services using video conferencing software such as Zoom or Skype. Tutors can create accounts for the following sites and schedule sessions with students by sending them the link to join the meeting. :

1. Zoom is a video conferencing software that allows tutors to conduct online tutoring sessions with students. Why - It is a reliable and easy-to-use platform that supports high-quality audio and video.

2. Skype is a video conferencing software that allows tutors to conduct online tutoring sessions with students. Why - It is a popular and widely-used platform that supports high-quality audio and video.

3. Google Meet is a video conferencing software that allows tutors to conduct online tutoring sessions with students. Why - It is a free and easy-to-use platform that supports high-quality audio and video.

4. Microsoft Teams is a video conferencing software that allows tutors to conduct online tutoring sessions with students. Why - It is a reliable and feature-rich platform that supports high-quality audio and video.

5. WizIQ is a virtual classroom software that allows tutors to conduct online tutoring sessions with students. Why - It is a comprehensive platform that supports a range of features, such as whiteboarding, document sharing, and recording.

6. GoToMeeting is a video conferencing software that allows tutors to conduct online tutoring sessions with students. Why - It is a reliable and secure platform that supports high-quality audio and video.

7. BlueJeans is a video conferencing software that allows tutors to conduct online tutoring sessions with students. Why - It is a user-friendly and flexible platform that supports a range of devices and platforms.

8. Cisco Webex is a video conferencing software that allows tutors to conduct online tutoring sessions with students. Why - It is a reliable and feature-rich platform that supports high-quality audio and video.

9. Zoho Meeting is a video conferencing software that allows tutors to conduct online tutoring sessions with students. Why - It is a cost-effective and easy-to-use platform that supports high-quality audio and video.

10. Join.me is a video conferencing software that allows tutors to conduct online tutoring sessions with students. Why - It is a simple and user-friendly platform that supports high-quality audio and video.

In conclusion, offering online tutoring services using video conferencing software is a powerful tool for tutoring businesses looking to expand their reach and provide high-quality services to students around the world. By investing in the necessary equipment and software, advertising their services effectively, and creating a structured and engaging learning environment, tutors can attract new clients, build strong relationships with existing clients, and ultimately grow their business.

Utilizing online directories, such as Yelp and Google My Business, to improve your local search engine rankings and attract new clients

Online directories, such as Yelp and Google My Business, offer businesses the opportunity to improve their local search engine rankings and attract new clients. By creating a listing on these directories and optimizing it with accurate and up-to-date information, tutoring businesses can increase their visibility to potential customers searching for services in their local area.

Utilizing online directories can be a valuable tool for tutoring businesses looking to expand their client base and reach a wider audience. By improving local search engine rankings, businesses can increase their visibility to potential customers and improve their chances of being found online. Additionally, online directories often provide features such as reviews and ratings, which can help to build trust and credibility with potential clients.

To utilize online directories effectively, tutoring businesses should first identify which directories are most relevant to their target audience and industry. Yelp and Google My Business are two popular directories particularly useful for tutoring businesses. Once identified, businesses should create a listing on each directory and optimize it with accurate and up-to-date information, including business hours, services offered, and contact information. Additionally, businesses should encourage clients to leave reviews on their listings, as positive reviews can help to improve search engine rankings and attract new clients. Overall, by utilizing online directories, tutoring businesses can improve their local search engine rankings and attract new clients, ultimately contributing to the growth and success of their business.

Here are several online directories that can be used in a tutoring business, along with a brief explanation of what they are, why they are important, and how to use them effectively:

1. Google My Business - A free tool provided by Google that allows businesses to manage their online presence across Google, including Search and Maps. This is important because it helps businesses show up in local search results and provides important information to potential clients, such as hours, phone numbers, and reviews.

2. Yelp - An online directory that allows users to search for and review businesses. This is important because it is a trusted source for local recommendations and can improve a business's visibility in search results.

3. Yellow Pages - An online directory that allows businesses to create a profile and be listed in the Yellow Pages directory. This is important because it is a well-known and trusted source for finding local businesses.

4. Angie's - A membership-based directory that allows users to search for and review businesses. This is important because it is a trusted source for local recommendations and can improve a business's visibility in search results.

5. Thumbtack - An online platform that connects service

professionals with customers. This is important because it provides a way for businesses to get their services in front of potential clients and receive leads directly.

6. Fiverr - An online marketplace that allows businesses to find freelancers for a variety of services. This is important because it can provide access to talented professionals who can help with things like website design, content creation, and marketing.

7. Bark - An online platform that connects businesses with service professionals. This is important because it provides a way for businesses to find professionals for a variety of services, including marketing, web design, and more.

Overall, utilizing online directories can be a great way for tutoring businesses to improve their local search engine rankings, attract new clients, and build their online presence. By creating a profile on these directories and actively managing and responding to reviews, businesses can improve their visibility and reputation, ultimately leading to more success in their industry.

In today's digital age, establishing a strong online presence is essential for any tutoring business. From developing a professional website that showcases your services and expertise to create a blog or resource center that offers valuable educational content for your target market, there are many ways to establish your brand online. Social media platforms such as Facebook, Instagram, and Twitter provide a powerful way to connect with potential clients and promote your services, while video conferencing software like Zoom or Skype allows for online tutoring services. Lastly, utilizing online directories like Yelp and Google My Business can improve your local search engine rankings and attract new clients. By implementing these strategies, you can take your tutoring business to new heights and reach a wider audience than ever before.

Chapter Eight

Building a Referral Network

In the world of tutoring business, referrals from satisfied clients and other professionals in your network can be the key to success. However, building a strong referral network takes more than just offering excellent tutoring services. It requires developing meaningful relationships with other professionals and fostering a culture of excellence and client satisfaction within your own business. In this chapter, we will explore some essential tips for building a strong referral network that can help you attract new clients and establish yourself as a trusted and respected provider of educational services. From developing relationships with other professionals to providing incentives for client referrals, we will cover everything you need to know to build a successful referral network and take your tutoring business to new heights.

One of the most effective ways to attract new clients to your tutoring business is through referrals from satisfied clients and other professionals in your network. Building a strong referral network involves developing relationships with other professionals and creating a culture of excellence and client satisfaction in your own business.

The following are several tips for building a strong referral network:

Offer exceptional tutoring services and consistently exceed client expectations. What does it mean to offer exceptional tutoring services? Why is it important to consistently exceed client expectations?

Exceptional tutoring services involve going above and beyond to ensure that your clients receive the highest quality of educational services. This means creating a personalized approach that meets each client's unique needs, utilizing the latest teaching techniques and technologies, and fostering a positive and supportive learning environment.

Consistently exceeding client expectations is important because it helps to build a strong reputation for your business and increase client satisfaction and loyalty. When clients feel that they are receiving exceptional services, they are more likely to recommend your business to others and become repeat clients themselves.

To offer exceptional tutoring services and consistently exceed client expectations, consider implementing the following tips:

1. Conduct a thorough assessment of each client's needs and learning style to develop a personalized approach to tutoring.
2. Utilize a variety of teaching techniques and technologies to create engaging and effective learning experiences.

3. Provide regular progress updates and feedback to clients and their families to ensure that they are aware of their progress and can make informed decisions about their educational journey.

4. Create a positive and supportive learning environment that fosters a love of learning and encourages clients to reach their full potential.

By offering exceptional tutoring services and consistently exceeding client expectations, you can set your business apart from the competition and establish a reputation for excellence in the field of education.

Develop strong relationships with other professionals, such as teachers, counselors, and educational consultants, who can refer clients to your business

Developing strong relationships with other professionals, such as teachers, counselors, and educational consultants, is a key strategy for building a referral network for your tutoring business. By building these relationships, you can tap into their networks and gain access to potential clients who are in need of your services.

Working with other professionals can be a win-win situation. You can provide value to their clients by offering supplementary educational services, while they can provide value to your business by referring clients to you. By developing strong relationships with other professionals, you can build a network of trusted colleagues who can help you grow your business.

Here are some tips for building relationships with other professionals:

1. Attend local events, such as educational conferences, seminars, and workshops, to network with other professionals in your field.
2. Participate in online forums and discussion groups for professionals in your industry.
3. Reach out to other professionals in your community and offer to collaborate on projects or events.
4. Join professional associations or organizations that cater to your industry, and attend their meetings and events.
5. Be generous with your time and expertise, and offer to help other professionals whenever possible.

By following these tips, you can develop strong relationships with other professionals and build a referral network to help you grow your tutoring business. Remember, building relationships takes time and effort, but the rewards are well worth it in the end.

Provide incentives for current clients to refer new clients to your business, such as discounted rates or referral bonuses

Providing incentives for current clients to refer new clients to your tutoring business is a powerful way to boost your referrals and expand your client base. Referral programs can include discounted rates or referral bonuses for clients who refer friends, family, or colleagues to your tutoring business.

Referral programs are an effective way to generate new business while also rewarding your current clients for their loyalty and trust. Offering referral incentives can also help create a sense of community and appreciation among your clients.

To implement a referral program in your tutoring business, consider offering discounted rates or referral bonuses to clients who refer new businesses to you. You can also use referral tracking software, such as Refersion, Ambassador, OSI Affiliate Software, or TapMango, to help you manage and track your referrals, making it easy to provide rewards to clients who refer new business to you. When designing your referral program, be sure to clearly communicate the incentives and requirements to your clients, and consider offering different levels of rewards for different levels of referrals. For example, you might offer a smaller discount or bonus for one referral and a larger reward for multiple referrals.

Incentivizing your clients to refer new business to your tutoring business can be a powerful way to build your client base and reward your current clients for their loyalty and trust. With the right incentives and clear communication, you can create a referral program that drives growth and helps to create a strong sense of community among your clients.

Participate in local events, such as educational conferences and community fairs, to network with other professionals and promote your services

Participating in local events, such as educational conferences and community fairs, can be an effective way to network with other professionals and promote your tutoring services.

Local events provide an opportunity to connect with other professionals and potential clients in your community. By attending educational conferences and community fairs, you can showcase your expertise and build relationships with other professionals who may refer clients to your business.

To make the most of local events, it's important to prepare ahead of time. Research the event and its attendees, and consider bringing marketing materials, such as business cards or brochures, to distribute to potential clients and partners. Consider offering a special promotion or discount to attendees who sign up for your tutoring services during the event. Finally, make an effort to engage with other professionals and attendees and follow up with any new connections after the event to continue building relationships. By participating in local events and networking with other professionals, you can expand your client base and build a strong reputation in your community as a trusted provider of educational services.

In conclusion, building a strong referral network for your tutoring business takes time, effort, and a commitment to excellence. By consistently exceeding client expectations and developing strong relationships with other professionals, you can build a network of trusted colleagues who can refer clients to your business. Additionally, offering incentives for current clients to refer new clients and participating in local events can help to expand your client base and build your reputation as a leader in the field of education. Remember, building a referral network is an ongoing process that requires continuous effort and attention, but the rewards can be significant. By implementing the strategies outlined in this chapter, you can take your tutoring business to new heights and achieve long-term success.

Chapter Nine

Setting Prices and Payment Policies

Setting prices and payment policies is a crucial part of running a successful tutoring business. It's not just about making money - it's about striking the right balance between affordability and quality to attract and retain clients. But how do you set prices that reflect the value of your services while also remaining competitive in your local market? In this chapter, we'll explore the factors that go into setting prices and payment policies for tutoring services. From considering demand and competition to assessing expertise and resources, we'll cover everything you need to know to make informed decisions about pricing your services.

We'll also discuss the importance of establishing clear and fair payment policies that are easy to understand and communicate to your clients. Setting the right prices and payment policies can create a positive and transparent experience for your clients, build trust, and ultimately grow your business. So whether you're just starting out or looking to refine your pricing strategy, this chapter will provide you with the insights and tools you need to succeed in the competitive tutoring world. Let's dive in!

Setting prices and payment policies for your tutoring business can be a complex and challenging task. It's important to balance the need to generate revenue with the need to provide affordable and accessible services to your target market.

Some factors to consider when setting prices and payment policies include the following:

The level of demand for your services and the competitive landscape in your local market

Understanding the level of demand for your tutoring services and the competitive landscape in your local market is essential when it comes to setting prices and payment policies for your business. If there is a high demand for your services and little competition, you may be able to charge higher prices and set more stringent payment policies. Conversely, if there is low demand and high competition, you may need to offer more affordable prices and flexible payment options to attract clients.

Here are some tips for understanding the level of demand for your services and the competitive landscape in your local market:

1. Conduct market research to understand the needs and preferences of your target market. Consider surveying potential clients to gain insight into their needs and price sensitivity.

2. Analyze your competition to understand their pricing and payment policies. This can help you to set competitive prices and payment policies that attract clients and remain

profitable.

3. Consider the unique value your business offers, such as personalized attention, expertise, or flexibility. Use this information to set prices that reflect the value of your services and distinguish your business from competitors.

By understanding the level of demand for your services and the competitive landscape in your local market, you can set prices and payment policies that attract clients while also ensuring the financial health of your business. Remember to continually evaluate your pricing and payment policies and adjust them as needed to remain competitive in your market.

The level of expertise and experience required to provide your services

What sets your tutoring business apart from others in the market? It's the level of expertise and experience you bring to the table. Whether you specialize in a particular subject area or offer a wide range of educational services, your level of expertise and experience is a key factor in determining the value of your services and the prices you can charge.

When setting prices for your services, it's important to consider the level of expertise and experience required to provide those services. For example, if you offer advanced math tutoring services, you may be able to charge a higher rate than a general academic tutor who provides homework help across a variety of subjects.

Your level of expertise and experience can also be a major selling point when marketing your services. Consider highlighting your qualifications, certifications, and educational background in your marketing materials, such as your website, brochures, and business cards. By showcasing your expertise and experience, you can differentiate your business from competitors and establish yourself as a trusted and knowledgeable provider of educational services.

It's important to remember that your expertise and experience can also impact the type of clients you attract. For example, if you specialize in advanced math tutoring, you may attract clients who are looking for highly specialized and focused services. On the other hand, if you provide more general academic support, you may attract a wider range of clients with varying needs and goals.

In order to provide the highest quality services to your clients, it's important to continue developing and refining your expertise and experience over time. Consider attending professional development workshops or conferences, pursuing additional certifications or degrees, or partnering with other professionals in your field to expand your knowledge and skill set. By staying up-to-date on the latest trends and techniques in your field, you can continue to provide exceptional services to your clients and set yourself apart as a leader in your industry.

The type of services you offer, such as one-on-one tutoring, group tutoring, or online tutoring

What type of tutoring services you offer can significantly impact your pricing and payment policies. Each type of tutoring service has its own unique benefits and challenges, and it's important to consider these factors when setting prices and payment policies. One-on-one tutoring services typically command higher prices due to the personalized attention and customized approach that they offer. However, they can also be more time-intensive and require more specialized expertise, impacting pricing. Group tutoring services, on the other hand, can be more cost-effective for clients and require less specialized expertise but may not offer the same level of personalized attention as one-on-one tutoring.

Online tutoring services are becoming increasingly popular due to their convenience and flexibility. They can also be more cost-effective for clients, as they eliminate the need for travel and can be conducted from the comfort of one's own home. However, they may also require specialized technology and software and may not be suitable for all clients, particularly those who require hands-on, in-person instruction.

When setting prices and payment policies for different types of tutoring services, it's important to consider the level of expertise and resources required, as well as the preferences and financial constraints of your target market. You can attract a broader range of clients and build a successful tutoring business by offering a range of services and pricing options.

The cost of any materials or resources required to provide your services

The cost of any materials or resources required to provide your tutoring services is important to consider when setting prices for your business. These costs can include textbooks, workbooks, software, and other materials necessary to provide high-quality educational services.

Understanding the costs of materials and resources is crucial for creating a sustainable business model. If you price your services too low, you may not be able to cover the costs of the materials and resources needed to provide those services. On the other hand, if you price your services too high, you may not be able to attract enough clients to sustain your business.

To determine the cost of materials and resources required to provide your tutoring services, consider the following factors:

1. Identify the materials and resources required for each service

you offer. For example, one-on-one tutoring may require textbooks and workbooks, while group tutoring may require additional materials such as whiteboards or projectors.

2. Research the costs of the materials and resources you need. Look for competitive pricing and deals to ensure that you are getting the best value for your money.

3. Determine how often you need to replenish your supplies. Some materials may need to be replaced more frequently than others, so it's important to factor this into your overall costs.

4. Consider ways to reduce your material costs, such as purchasing used textbooks or utilizing online resources. Be mindful, however, of the quality and reliability of these materials.

By carefully considering the costs of materials and resources required to provide your tutoring services, you can set fair and reasonable prices that reflect the value of your services while also ensuring the sustainability of your business.

The preferences and financial constraints of your target market

Your target market's preferences and financial constraints can greatly impact your tutoring business's pricing and payment policies.

Understanding your target market's preferences and financial constraints is essential to providing affordable and accessible services while also generating revenue for your business. Failing to consider these factors can result in setting prices and payment policies that are out of reach for your target market, leading to a loss of potential clients and revenue.

To better understand your target market's preferences and financial constraints, consider conducting market research or surveys to gather data on their needs and expectations. This can include factors such as their preferred learning style, the amount they are willing to pay for tutoring services, and any financial assistance programs they may be eligible for. Use this information to develop pricing and payment policies that are both fair to your business and accessible to your target market.

When setting prices, consider offering tiered pricing options that cater to clients with different financial constraints. For example, you may offer a basic package for clients on a tight budget, with fewer services or less personalized attention, and a premium package for clients who are willing to pay more for additional services or attention. This allows clients to choose a pricing option that best fits their financial situation while still receiving the educational support they need.

In addition to tiered pricing, consider offering flexible payment options, such as payment plans or sliding-scale fees based on income. This can help make your services more accessible to clients who may not have the financial means to pay upfront for tutoring services.

By understanding the preferences and financial constraints of your target market and developing pricing and payment policies that cater to them, you can attract more clients and generate more revenue while also providing affordable and accessible services.

In conclusion, setting prices and payment policies for your tutoring business is a critical aspect of its success. It's important to consider a variety of factors, including the level of demand for your services, the competitive landscape in your local market, the level of expertise and experience required to provide your services, the type of services you offer, and the cost of any materials or resources required. Additionally, it's essential to understand the preferences and financial constraints of your target market to ensure that your pricing and payment policies are fair, reasonable, and accessible. By carefully considering these factors and continually evaluating and adjusting your pricing strategy as needed, you can create a sustainable and successful tutoring business that meets the needs of your clients and community.

Chapter Ten
Managing Finances and Taxes

Welcome to Chapter 10: Managing Finances and Taxes. As a small business owner, you know that managing your finances and taxes is crucial to the success of your tutoring business. Without a solid financial plan and a thorough understanding of tax laws and regulations, it's easy to fall behind on payments, miss out on deductions, and even face legal consequences.

In this chapter, we'll explore the key principles of managing finances and taxes for your tutoring business. From creating a financial plan to keeping accurate records and complying with tax laws, we'll cover everything you need to know to keep your business financially healthy and thriving.

We'll start by discussing the importance of developing a financial plan for your business. By projecting your revenue, expenses, and profits, you can make informed decisions about pricing, marketing, and investments, and avoid the risk of overspending or underselling your services. We'll also cover the importance of creating a budget and monitoring your expenses regularly to stay on track with your financial plan.

Next, we'll dive into the nitty-gritty of financial record-keeping, including the importance of keeping accurate records of all financial transactions, from income and expenses to taxes and deductions. We'll discuss the pros and cons of using accounting software versus hiring a bookkeeper or accountant to manage your financial records, and provide tips for staying organized and up-to-date on your financial obligations.

Finally, we'll discuss tax laws and regulations that apply to tutoring businesses, including income taxes, sales taxes, and employment taxes. We'll cover the basics of these tax laws and provide tips for ensuring compliance and minimizing your tax liability.

By the end of this chapter, you'll have a comprehensive understanding of how to manage your finances and taxes as a small business owner. Whether you're just starting out or looking to refine your financial management skills, this chapter will provide you with the insights and tools you need to succeed in the competitive world of tutoring. Let's get started!

As a small business owner, it's important to manage your finances and taxes effectively to ensure the long-term success of your tutoring business. This involves developing a financial plan, keeping accurate records, and complying with all relevant tax laws and regulations.

Some tips for managing finances and taxes in your tutoring business include:

Develop a financial plan that includes projected revenue,

expenses, and profit

Developing a financial plan is an essential step in managing your tutoring business's finances effectively. It provides a roadmap for your business's financial future and helps you make informed decisions about spending, investing, and growing your business. When developing a financial plan, it's important to consider several key factors, including projected revenue, expenses, and profit. Revenue refers to the total amount of money that your business expects to generate from its tutoring services. Expenses, on the other hand, refer to the costs associated with running your business, such as rent, utilities, salaries, and supplies. Profit is the difference between your revenue and expenses and is a measure of your business's financial success.

To develop a financial plan for your tutoring business, start by projecting your revenue for the upcoming year. This can be based on your historical sales data or market research on the demand for tutoring services in your area. Be sure to consider any seasonality or fluctuations in demand for your services throughout the year.

Next, identify your expenses, including both fixed and variable costs. Fixed costs are expenses that remain the same each month, such as rent and insurance, while variable costs fluctuate depending on your business's activity, such as marketing and advertising expenses.

Once you have projected your revenue and expenses, calculate your expected profit for the upcoming year. This will give you a clear understanding of your business's financial position and help you make informed decisions about future investments or spending.

It's important to review and update your financial plan regularly to ensure that it remains accurate and relevant to your business's current financial situation. Consider conducting a quarterly review to assess your progress toward your revenue and profit goals and make any necessary adjustments to your financial plan.

By developing a financial plan that includes projected revenue, expenses, and profit, you can take control of your tutoring business's finances and make informed decisions about its future growth and success.

Creating a budget and monitoring your expenses regularly to ensure that you stay within your financial plan

Creating a budget and monitoring your expenses is an essential part of managing your tutoring business finances. A budget is a financial plan that outlines your expected revenue and expenses for a given period, typically a month or a year. It helps you to anticipate your cash flow and ensure that you have enough funds to cover your expenses and meet your financial goals.

To create a budget, start by listing all of your expected revenue streams, such as tutoring fees, grants, or sponsorships. Next, list all of your anticipated expenses, such as rent, utilities, office supplies, and marketing costs. Be sure to include both fixed expenses, such as rent and salaries, and variable expenses, such as marketing and supplies.

Once you have identified your revenue and expenses, calculate your projected profit by subtracting your expenses from your revenue. This will give you a clear idea of your financial position and help you to determine whether your tutoring business is profitable or if you need to make adjustments to your expenses or revenue streams.

It's important to regularly monitor your expenses and compare them to your budget to ensure that you stay on track. This can help you to identify areas where you may be overspending or underperforming in terms of revenue. You can use financial management software or spreadsheets to track your expenses and compare them to your budget.

If you find that you are overspending in certain areas or not generating as much revenue as expected, consider making adjustments to your budget. This may include reducing expenses, increasing revenue streams, or changing your pricing or marketing strategy.

By creating a budget and regularly monitoring your expenses, you can stay on top of your finances and make informed decisions that support the long-term success of your tutoring business.

Keeping accurate records of all financial transactions, including income, expenses, and taxes

Keeping accurate financial records is a critical component of managing the finances of your tutoring business. It enables you to track your income, expenses, and taxes, and provides you with valuable insights into the financial health of your business. By maintaining accurate financial records, you can make informed decisions, identify areas for improvement, and ensure compliance with tax laws and regulations.

There are several types of financial records that you should keep, including:

1. Income records: These records should include all sources of income for your tutoring business, such as payments from clients, grants, or sponsorships.
2. Expense records: Keep track of all expenses related to your tutoring business, including rent, supplies, equipment, travel expenses, and salaries.
3. Tax records: These records should include all documents related to your tax filings, such as receipts, invoices, and

bank statements.

To maintain accurate financial records, consider using accounting software or hiring a bookkeeper or accountant to help you manage your finances. This can help to streamline the process and ensure that all financial records are accurate and up-to-date.

In addition to keeping accurate records, it's important to regularly review your financial records to identify any discrepancies or errors. By regularly reviewing your records, you can catch any errors early on and take corrective action before they become bigger problems.

Overall, keeping accurate financial records is essential for the success of your tutoring business. It enables you to make informed decisions, ensure compliance with tax laws and regulations, and identify areas for improvement. By prioritizing financial record-keeping, you can set your business up for long-term financial stability and success.

Utilizing accounting software or hiring a bookkeeper or accountant to manage your financial records and taxes.

Utilizing accounting software or hiring a bookkeeper or accountant to manage your financial records and taxes is essential to maintaining the financial health and stability of your tutoring business. While it may seem daunting to entrust your financial records and taxes to someone else, hiring a professional or using accounting software can actually save you time, money, and stress in the long run.

One of the main benefits of using accounting software or hiring a professional is that they can help you stay organized and up-to-date with your financial records. This includes tracking income, expenses, and taxes, as well as generating reports and statements that can help you make informed financial decisions for your business. They can also help you identify areas where you can save money or cut expenses, as well as provide guidance on how to optimize your business finances.

Additionally, utilizing accounting software or hiring a professional can help you stay in compliance with tax laws and regulations. Tax laws can be complex and constantly changing, so it's important to have someone on your side who is knowledgeable and up-to-date with the latest regulations. This can help you avoid costly mistakes or penalties and ensure that you are taking advantage of all possible deductions and credits.

When considering whether to use accounting software or hire a professional, it's important to weigh the costs and benefits. While there is an initial investment involved in hiring a professional or purchasing accounting software, the long-term benefits can outweigh the costs in terms of time saved, stress reduced, and financial stability achieved. Additionally, some accounting software options are affordable and user-friendly, making them a great option for small businesses with limited budgets.

Ultimately, utilizing accounting software or hiring a professional can help you manage your finances and taxes more effectively, giving you more time and energy to focus on providing high-quality tutoring services to your clients.

Complying with all relevant tax laws and regulations, including income taxes, sales taxes, and employment taxes

Complying with tax laws and regulations is crucial for small business owners to avoid penalties and legal issues. It involves understanding and following all relevant tax laws and regulations, including income taxes, sales taxes, and employment taxes.

Failure to comply with tax laws and regulations can result in penalties, fines, legal action, and damage to your business's reputation. Compliance can also ensure that you are taking advantage of all available tax deductions and credits, which can help reduce your tax burden.

To comply with tax laws and regulations, small business owners should stay up to date on any changes or updates to tax laws, keep accurate and complete financial records, file and pay taxes on time, and seek advice from a tax professional if necessary. It is also important to understand the different tax requirements for different types of businesses and industries. By taking the necessary steps to comply with tax laws and regulations, small business owners can protect their business and ensure its long-term success.

In conclusion, managing finances and taxes is a critical aspect of running a successful tutoring business. By developing a financial plan, creating a budget, keeping accurate financial records, utilizing accounting software or hiring a bookkeeper or accountant, and complying with tax laws and regulations, small business owners can ensure the financial health and stability of their businesses. It can seem overwhelming at first, but by taking the time to understand and implement these key principles, small business owners can make informed financial decisions and achieve long-term success. Remember to regularly review and update your financial plan, budget, and records, and seek advice from professionals when necessary. With dedication and careful attention to your finances, you can ensure the success and growth of your tutoring business.

Chapter Eleven

Hiring and Managing Tutors

Welcome to Chapter 11: Hiring and Managing Tutors. As your tutoring business grows, you may find that you need to expand your team and bring on additional tutors to meet the demand for your services. However, hiring and managing tutors effectively is not just about finding people to fill a position. It's about creating a team of highly skilled professionals who share your vision and commitment to providing high-quality educational services.

This chapter will explore the key principles of hiring and managing tutors for your tutoring business. From developing a clear job description and selection criteria to providing ongoing training and support, we'll cover everything you need to know to create a team of exceptional tutors who can help your business thrive.

We'll start by discussing the importance of developing a clear job description and selection criteria for your tutors. This involves identifying the skills, qualifications, and experience necessary for a successful tutor in your business, as well as defining your expectations for their role in your business.

Next, we'll dive into the selection process, which includes conducting thorough interviews and background checks to ensure that your tutors meet your standards and are a good fit for your business. We'll provide tips for conducting effective interviews and identifying the qualities that make a great tutor.

Once you've hired your tutors, we'll discuss the importance of ongoing training and support to ensure they have the skills and knowledge necessary to provide quality tutoring services. This includes regular check-ins, professional development opportunities, and feedback and performance evaluations.

Effective communication and management are also crucial to successfully hiring and managing tutors. We'll discuss the importance of communicating clear expectations and providing regular feedback and evaluations to your tutors to ensure they meet your business's standards and goals.

Finally, we'll explore the importance of developing a competitive compensation and benefits package that rewards excellence and dedication. This can help you attract and retain top-quality tutors and ensure that your clients receive the highest level of educational services and satisfaction.

By the end of this chapter, you'll have a comprehensive understanding of how to hire and manage top-quality tutors for your tutoring business. Whether you're just starting out or looking to expand your team, this chapter will provide you with the insights and tools you need to create a team of exceptional tutors who can help your business thrive. Let's get started!

As your tutoring business grows, you may need to hire

additional tutors to help meet the demand for your services. Hiring and managing tutors effectively involves a careful selection process, ongoing training and support, and effective management and communication.

Some tips for hiring and managing tutors in your tutoring business include:

Developing a clear job description and selection criteria for your tutors

Developing a clear job description and selection criteria for your tutors is crucial in ensuring that you hire the right people to join your tutoring team. A well-written job description can help you attract high-quality candidates, while clear selection criteria can help you identify the best fit for your business.

A job description should outline the key responsibilities and requirements of the tutoring position, including educational background, tutoring experience, subject matter expertise, and any specific skills or certifications required. It should also include information on the position's schedule, compensation, and benefits.

In addition to outlining the position's basic requirements, a job description should also highlight the values and mission of your tutoring business. This can help to attract candidates who share your passion for education and are committed to providing quality tutoring services.

Once you have developed a clear job description, it's important to establish selection criteria that will help you identify the best fit for your business. This can include evaluating candidates based on their education, tutoring experience, and communication and interpersonal skills. It may also include conducting interviews and reference checks to better understand each candidate's personality and work style.

To ensure you hire the best possible candidates, it's important to take a comprehensive and thorough approach to the selection process. This can include screening resumes, conducting multiple rounds of interviews, and checking references to verify the candidate's qualifications and suitability for the position.

By developing a clear job description and selection criteria, you can attract and hire top-quality tutors committed to providing your clients the highest level of educational services. This can help to establish your tutoring business as a leader in the industry and ensure its long-term success.

Looking to hire top-quality tutors for your tutoring business? The following sample job descriptions may provide a template for writing your own job descriptions:

Job Description: Foreign Language Tutor

We are seeking an experienced and knowledgeable foreign language tutor to join our tutoring team. The successful candidate will be responsible for providing one-on-one and small group tutoring sessions to students of all ages and skill levels in a variety of foreign languages, including but not limited to Spanish, French, and Mandarin.

Responsibilities:

- Develop individualized tutoring plans for each student based on their skill level and learning style
- Provide engaging and interactive tutoring sessions to improve students' reading, writing, listening, and speaking skills
- Track and report on student progress and provide regular feedback to parents/guardians
- Develop and utilize effective teaching strategies and materials
- Stay up-to-date with current trends and best practices in foreign language instruction

Requirements:

- Bachelor's degree in a related field (linguistics, education, foreign language) preferred

- Previous experience in foreign language tutoring or teaching
- Strong communication and interpersonal skills
- Ability to work with students of varying ages and skill levels
- Ability to speak, read, and write fluently in one or more foreign languages
- Familiarity with the culture and customs of the target language(s) is a plus

Job Description: Math Tutor

We are seeking a dedicated and knowledgeable math tutor to join our tutoring team. The successful candidate will be responsible for providing one-on-one and small group tutoring sessions to students of all ages and skill levels in a variety of math subjects, including but not limited to algebra, geometry, calculus, and statistics.

Responsibilities:

- Develop individualized tutoring plans for each student based on their skill level and learning style
- Provide engaging and interactive tutoring sessions to improve students' understanding and mastery of math concepts and skills
- Track and report on student progress and provide regular feedback to parents/guardians
- Develop and utilize effective teaching strategies and

materials

- Stay up-to-date with current trends and best practices in math instruction

Requirements:

- Bachelor's degree in math, education, or a related field preferred
- Previous experience in math tutoring or teaching
- Strong communication and interpersonal skills
- Ability to work with students of varying ages and skill levels
- Ability to teach a variety of math subjects, including algebra, geometry, calculus, and statistics
- Familiarity with common math curricula and standardized tests such as the SAT and ACT is a plus

Job Description: SAT Tutor

We are seeking a skilled and experienced SAT tutor to join our tutoring team. The successful candidate will be responsible for providing one-on-one and small-group tutoring sessions to students preparing for the SAT exam.

Responsibilities:

- Develop individualized tutoring plans for each student based on their strengths and weaknesses
- Provide engaging and interactive tutoring sessions to

improve students' understanding and mastery of the SAT content and format

- Teach strategies for test-taking and time management
- Track and report on student progress and provide regular feedback to parents/guardians
- Develop and utilize effective teaching strategies and materials
- Stay up-to-date with current trends and best practices in SAT preparation

Requirements:

- Bachelor's degree in a related field (education, English, math) preferred
- Previous experience in SAT tutoring or teaching
- Strong communication and interpersonal skills
- Ability to work with students of varying ages and skill levels
- Ability to teach the content and format of the SAT exam, including reading, writing, and math sections
- Familiarity with the scoring and structure of the SAT exam is a plus

Developing a clear job description and selection criteria for your tutors is essential to ensure that you are hiring the right people to join your tutoring team. A well-written job description can help you attract high-quality candidates, while clear selection criteria can help you identify the best fit for your business. By taking a comprehensive and thorough approach to the selection process and hiring top-quality tutors, you can establish your tutoring business as a leader in the industry and ensure its long-term success. Remember, hiring and managing top-quality tutors is a key factor in providing the highest level of educational services and satisfaction to your clients.

Conducting thorough interviews and background checks to ensure that your tutors meet your standards and are a good fit for your business

Conducting thorough interviews and background checks is an essential part of the tutor selection process. By doing so, you can ensure that the candidates you select are qualified and have the necessary skills to provide quality tutoring services.

The purpose of conducting interviews is to get to know the candidate better, assess their qualifications, and determine if they are a good fit for your business. During the interview process, it's important to ask questions to help you understand the candidate's experience, teaching style, and ability to communicate effectively with students.

It's also important to conduct a background check to verify the candidate's credentials, such as their educational background and previous employment history. A thorough background check can help you identify any red flags or potential issues that may impact their ability to provide quality tutoring services.

In addition to verifying their credentials, it's important to assess the candidate's personality and work style to ensure that they are a good fit for your tutoring business. This can include evaluating their communication skills, their ability to work well with others, and their overall professionalism.

Here are some interview questions based on conducting thorough interviews and background checks for tutoring candidates:

1. What motivated you to pursue a career in tutoring, and how did you get started in this field?
2. How do you approach developing a customized tutoring plan for each student, and what strategies have you found to be most effective in improving student performance?
3. How do you assess student progress and provide feedback to parents and guardians, and what methods do you use to track student learning and achievement?
4. What techniques do you use to engage and motivate students who may be struggling with a particular subject or topic?
5. How do you stay up-to-date with current trends and best practices in education and tutoring, and what resources do you rely on for professional development?
6. Can you provide an example of a time when you had to

handle a difficult or challenging student, and how did you manage the situation?

7. What do you believe are the most important qualities of a successful tutor, and how do you embody these qualities in your work?

8. How do you ensure that you provide a safe and supportive learning environment for all students, regardless of their background or learning style?

9. Can you describe your experience working with students from diverse cultural or linguistic backgrounds, and how do you adapt your teaching approach to meet their unique needs?

10. Finally, can you tell us about any relevant certifications or training you have completed and how these credentials enhance your ability to provide quality tutoring services?

Ultimately, conducting thorough interviews and background checks aims to select the best candidates for your tutoring team. By doing so, you can ensure that your clients receive the highest level of educational services and satisfaction.

Providing ongoing training and support to your tutors to ensure that they have the skills and knowledge necessary to provide quality tutoring services

Providing ongoing training and support to your tutors is

essential in ensuring they have the skills and knowledge necessary to provide quality tutoring services. This not only benefits your tutors but also ensures that your clients receive the highest level of educational services.

Training should begin with an orientation session that introduces tutors to your tutoring business's values, mission, policies, and procedures. This session should also provide an overview of your tutoring services and the expectations for tutors' roles and responsibilities.

In addition to the orientation session, ongoing training should be provided to ensure that tutors stay up-to-date with the latest teaching strategies and best practices in their subject areas. This can include workshops, professional development sessions, and access to educational resources.

Regular communication and feedback are also essential in providing ongoing support to your tutors. This can include regular check-ins, performance evaluations, and constructive feedback on their tutoring sessions. Tutors should also be encouraged to share their experiences and feedback to help improve their tutoring services continually.

The following are some possible training topics for tutoring staff:

1. Effective tutoring techniques and strategies for different

subjects and grade levels

2. Classroom management and student engagement

3. Learning styles and how to tailor tutoring sessions to meet individual student needs

4. Assessing student progress and adjusting instruction accordingly

5. Developing lesson plans and materials

6. Technology integration in tutoring sessions

7. Understanding and accommodating learning disabilities and special needs

8. Culturally responsive teaching and addressing diverse student populations

9. Best practices for communicating with parents and guardians

10. Professional development and staying up-to-date with current trends and research in education.

Overall, providing ongoing training and support to your tutors not only benefits your tutoring business but also benefits your tutors and clients. By investing in your tutors' professional development, you can ensure that they have the necessary skills and knowledge to provide quality tutoring services and contribute to the success of your tutoring business.

Communicating clear expectations and providing regular

feedback and performance evaluations to your tutors

Communicating clear expectations and providing regular feedback and performance evaluations are essential for the success of your tutoring business. As a tutor manager, you must ensure that your tutors understand what is expected of them and how they can improve their performance.

Communicating clear expectations means you must clearly define each tutor's role and responsibilities. This includes expectations around the quality of tutoring services, communication with clients, scheduling, and administrative tasks. Establishing expectations around behavior and conduct in the workplace is also important.

When tutors clearly understand what is expected of them, they are more likely to perform well and meet your standards. Clear expectations also help minimize misunderstandings and conflicts between tutors and clients, improving client satisfaction and retention.

Regular feedback and performance evaluations are key to ensuring your tutors meet your expectations and perform at their best. Feedback should be timely, specific, and constructive, highlighting strengths and improvement areas. Performance evaluations can be conducted on a regular basis, such as quarterly or annually, and should include a review of each tutor's performance against established expectations.

Establishing an open and honest line of communication with your tutors is also important. Encourage them to ask questions and provide feedback on their experiences working for your tutoring business. This can help to improve morale, foster a sense of community, and identify areas where you can improve your management practices.

In summary, communicating clear expectations and providing regular feedback and performance evaluations are essential for the success of your tutoring business. By doing so, you can help ensure that your tutors provide high-quality tutoring services and meet your standards while fostering a positive and productive work environment.

Develop a compensation and benefits package that is competitive and rewards excellence and dedication

Developing a competitive compensation and benefits package that rewards excellence and dedication is an essential part of building a successful tutoring business. It ensures that your tutors are motivated and feel valued for their hard work and dedication to providing quality educational services.

By offering competitive compensation and benefits, you can attract top-quality tutors and retain them over the long term. This can help to establish your business as a leader in the industry and ensure the success of your tutoring services.

When developing a compensation and benefits package, it's important to consider factors such as experience, education, and performance. This can include offering bonuses and incentives based on performance metrics and providing professional development and growth opportunities.

Additionally, it's important to offer competitive salaries and benefits packages that include health insurance, retirement plans, and paid time off. These benefits not only help attract and retain top talent but also show that you value your tutors' hard work and dedication.

Here are some examples of what could go into a compensation and benefits package for tutors:

1. **Competitive hourly rate:** A competitive hourly rate is one of the most important components of a compensation package. This will depend on factors such as the tutor's level of education and experience, as well as the subject matter they are tutoring.

2. **Performance-based bonuses:** To reward excellence and dedication, you may consider offering performance-based bonuses. These could be based on factors such as the tutor's student retention rate, student satisfaction ratings, or overall

performance.

3. **Flexible scheduling:** Tutors often appreciate the ability to set their own schedules, so consider offering flexible scheduling options. This could include the ability to work from home or to set their own hours.

4. **Professional development opportunities:** Continuing education and professional development are important for tutors to stay up-to-date with the latest teaching methods and subject matter expertise. Consider offering reimbursement for professional development courses, conferences, or workshops.

5. **Health and wellness benefits:** Providing health and wellness benefits can be a valuable addition to a compensation package. This could include options such as medical, dental, and vision insurance, as well as gym memberships or wellness programs.

6. **Retirement benefits:** Consider offering retirement benefits such as a 401(k) plan with matching contributions or a pension plan.

7. **Paid time off:** Tutors also appreciate time off, so consider offering paid time off options such as vacation days, sick days, or personal days.

By offering a competitive compensation and benefits package, you can create a positive work environment that motivates and rewards your tutors for their hard work and dedication. This can help build a strong team of tutors committed to providing quality educational services and driving the success of your tutoring business. By hiring and managing top-quality tutors, you can ensure that your clients receive the highest level of educational services and satisfaction.

As your tutoring business continues to grow, your team of tutors will be instrumental in providing high-quality educational services to your clients. Hiring and managing tutors is more than just filling a position; it's about creating a team of highly skilled professionals who share your vision and commitment to excellence.

This chapter explored the key principles of hiring and managing tutors for your tutoring business. We started by discussing the importance of developing a clear job description and selection criteria to identify the skills, qualifications, and experience necessary for a successful tutor in your business.

We then delved into the selection process, offering tips on conducting effective interviews and identifying the qualities that make a great tutor. We also discussed the importance of providing ongoing training and support to ensure that your tutors have the skills and knowledge necessary to provide quality tutoring services.

Effective communication and management are also crucial to successfully hiring and managing tutors. We highlighted the importance of communicating clear expectations and providing regular feedback and evaluations to your tutors to ensure they meet your business's standards and goals.

Finally, we explored the importance of developing a competitive compensation and benefits package that rewards excellence and dedication. By doing so, you can attract and retain top-quality tutors and ensure that your clients receive the highest level of educational services and satisfaction.

Chapter Twelve

Providing Quality Tutoring Services

Welcome to Chapter 12 on providing quality tutoring services. As a tutor, your main goal is to help your clients achieve their educational goals and reach their full potential. But how do you ensure that you are providing quality tutoring services that meet the unique needs of your clients?

This chapter will explore the key principles of providing quality tutoring services. From developing a personalized learning plan to incorporating assessments and feedback, we'll cover everything you need to know to provide your clients the highest level of educational services.

We'll start by discussing the importance of developing a personalized learning plan for each client. This involves identifying their specific needs and learning preferences, as well as their goals and expectations for tutoring services. By creating a customized learning plan, you can tailor your tutoring sessions to meet each client's unique needs and help them achieve their educational goals.

Next, we'll dive into the teaching strategies and materials that can help you engage and motivate your clients. From visual aids and technology to hands-on activities, we'll explore the variety of teaching methods available to tutors and how to choose the most effective ones for your clients.

Assessments and feedback are also crucial components of quality tutoring services. We'll discuss how to incorporate assessments into your tutoring sessions and provide feedback to your clients to track progress and identify areas for improvement.

Creating a positive and supportive learning environment is also important for quality tutoring services. We'll explore how to build a rapport with your clients and foster confidence and self-esteem in their learning process.

Finally, we'll discuss the importance of ongoing communication and support to ensure that your clients are satisfied with your services and making progress toward their educational goals. We'll provide tips for maintaining a strong relationship with your clients and their families.

By the end of this chapter, you'll have a comprehensive understanding of how to provide quality tutoring services that meet your client's unique needs and learning preferences. Whether you're just starting out or looking to improve your tutoring services, this chapter will provide you with the insights and tools you need to succeed. Let's get started!

Providing quality tutoring services is at the heart of any successful tutoring business. This involves developing a pedagogical approach that meets your client's unique needs and learning preferences and utilizing best practices in the field of education.

The following are some of the tips that you can use in your business to provide quality tutoring services include:

Developing a personalized learning plan for each client based on their specific needs and learning preferences

What is a personalized learning plan, and why is it important to provide quality tutoring services? A personalized learning plan is a tailored approach to education that takes into account the unique needs, learning styles, and preferences of each individual student. By developing a personalized learning plan for each client, tutors can create an environment that is conducive to learning and growth.

Why is this important? Traditional classroom settings often use a one-size-fits-all approach to education, which can leave some students struggling to keep up or feeling disengaged from the material. On the other hand, personalized learning plans can help students feel more invested in their education and lead to better outcomes.

How can you develop a personalized learning plan for your clients? Start by assessing each client's current level of knowledge and understanding in the subject area you will be tutoring. From there, work with the client to identify their learning style and preferences, as well as any specific areas where they need extra support or attention.

Once you clearly understand your client's needs and learning preferences, you can develop a tailored plan that includes specific goals, learning activities, and assessment strategies. This can help you ensure that each tutoring session focuses on meeting the needs of the individual client and that they are progressing towards their educational goals.

The following are two examples of personalized learning plans for different clients:

Example 1: Jane is a high school student who struggles with algebra. She has difficulty understanding the concepts and often feels frustrated and discouraged. After an initial assessment and consultation with Jane and her parents, her tutor developed a personalized learning plan that includes the following:

- Breaking down complex concepts into smaller, more manageable parts
- Providing real-world examples and visual aids to help Jane understand the material
- Developing a system for practicing problems and tracking progress
- Providing regular feedback and positive reinforcement to build Jane's confidence

Example 2: Tom is a college student who is preparing for the

GRE exam. He is a visual learner who enjoys interactive and hands-on activities. After an initial assessment and consultation with Tom, his tutor develops a personalized learning plan that includes the following:

- Incorporating visual aids such as diagrams and graphs to help Tom understand the material
- Utilizing interactive online tools and games to keep Tom engaged and motivated
- Providing opportunities for Tom to practice and apply the material through mock exams and quizzes
- Adjusting the pace and focus of the tutoring sessions based on Tom's progress and feedback.

By developing a personalized learning plan for each client, you can create a more effective and engaging tutoring experience that meets the unique needs of each individual student. This can lead to improved outcomes, increased confidence, and a greater sense of satisfaction for both you and your clients.

Utilizing a variety of teaching strategies and materials, such as visual aids, technology, and hands-on activities, to engage and motivate your clients

Utilizing a variety of teaching strategies and materials is a key element of providing quality tutoring services. By incorporating visual aids, technology, and hands-on activities into your tutoring sessions, you can help your clients engage with the material and stay motivated to learn.

Different clients have different learning preferences, and utilizing various teaching strategies and materials can help you accommodate these preferences and meet each client's unique needs. Furthermore, incorporating visual aids, technology, and hands-on activities can help make learning more enjoyable and memorable for your clients, ultimately leading to better outcomes.

To effectively utilize a variety of teaching strategies and materials, it's important to first assess your clients' learning preferences and needs. This can involve conducting an initial assessment or simply asking your clients about their preferred learning styles. Once you have a better understanding of their needs, you can start incorporating different teaching strategies and materials into your tutoring sessions.

For example, you might use visual aids such as diagrams, charts, and graphs to help clients learn better through visual cues. You could also incorporate technology such as educational apps, online learning platforms, or interactive whiteboards to provide a more interactive and engaging learning experience. Additionally, you could use hands-on activities such as experiments, games, or simulations to help clients learn better through kinesthetic or experiential learning.

By utilizing a variety of teaching strategies and materials, you can provide your clients with a personalized and engaging learning experience that is tailored to their specific needs and preferences.

Incorporating assessments and feedback into your tutoring sessions to track progress and identify areas for improvement

Incorporating assessments and feedback into your tutoring sessions is a crucial component of providing high-quality educational services. By regularly assessing your clients' progress and providing feedback, you can identify areas where they are excelling and areas where they may need additional support.

Assessments and feedback help keep your clients motivated and engaged in learning. By providing positive reinforcement for their achievements and identifying areas where they can improve, you can help them build confidence and improve their skills and knowledge. Additionally, assessments and feedback can help you as a tutor to track your clients' progress and adjust your teaching strategies and materials as needed. This can help you to better meet their unique needs and learning preferences, ultimately leading to better outcomes and greater success.

To incorporate assessments and feedback into your tutoring sessions, consider the following tips:

- Begin each session with a quick review of the previous session's material to gauge your client's retention and understanding.
- Utilize a variety of assessment tools, such as quizzes, tests, and interactive activities, to track progress and identify areas for improvement.
- Provide regular feedback on your client's performance, highlighting areas of strength and areas that require additional attention.
- Work with your client to set specific goals and benchmarks, and regularly review progress towards these goals.
- Use assessments and feedback as a tool for ongoing communication and collaboration with your clients and their families, keeping them informed and engaged in the learning process.

The following are a few examples of online platforms that can help with incorporating assessments and feedback into tutoring sessions:

1. Kahoot!: This online platform allows tutors to create interactive quizzes and games to engage their clients and track their progress. It provides instant feedback and

assessments, which can help tutors identify areas for improvement.

2. Quizlet: Quizlet is an online learning tool that allows tutors to create flashcards, study guides, and quizzes to assess their clients' knowledge and track their progress. It provides immediate feedback on answers and offers personalized study recommendations.

3. Google Forms: This free tool from Google allows tutors to create surveys and quizzes to gather feedback from their clients. Tutors can use this feedback to identify areas for improvement and adjust their teaching approach accordingly.

4. Edmentum Assessments: This comprehensive assessment program provides tutors with a wide range of pre-built assessments and customized assessment options. It offers immediate feedback and analysis, which can help tutors track progress and identify areas for improvement.

5. Zoom: This video conferencing software offers features such as screen sharing, virtual whiteboards, and chat options to help tutors incorporate assessments and feedback into their tutoring sessions. They can share educational materials and visually track their clients' progress while providing real-time feedback.

These are just a few examples of online platforms that can

help tutors incorporate assessments and feedback into their sessions. Researching and choosing the tools that best fit your tutoring business's needs and goals is important. By incorporating assessments and feedback into your tutoring sessions, you can help your clients achieve their educational goals and position your business as a leader in the field of education.

Developing a positive and supportive learning environment that fosters confidence and self-esteem in your clients

Developing a positive and supportive learning environment is crucial to the success of any tutoring session. A positive environment fosters confidence, motivation, and self-esteem in your clients, making them more receptive to learning and more likely to achieve their educational goals.

Creating a positive learning environment can significantly impact your clients' academic success. When clients feel supported, encouraged, and respected, they are more likely to engage in the learning process and take risks to challenge themselves. A positive environment can also help to alleviate anxiety and stress, which can be major barriers to learning.

You can use several strategies to create a positive and supportive learning environment for your clients. Here are a few ideas:

1. Build rapport: Take the time to get to know your clients, their interests, and their learning styles. Show genuine interest in their progress and accomplishments.

2. Provide positive feedback: Encourage and praise your clients for their efforts and progress and provide constructive feedback that helps them identify improvement areas.

3. Set realistic goals: Work with your clients to set achievable goals tailored to their needs and abilities.

4. Use positive language: Choose a positive and empowering language, and avoid using negative or critical language that can be demotivating.

5. Create a welcoming environment: Ensure your tutoring space is clean, organized, and welcoming. Use visual aids and other materials to make the space inviting and engaging.

By utilizing these strategies, you can create a positive and supportive learning environment that fosters confidence and self-esteem in your clients and helps them to achieve their educational goals.

Providing ongoing communication and support to your clients and their families to ensure that they are satisfied with your services and making progress toward their educational goals

Providing ongoing communication and support to your

clients and their families is essential to ensuring their satisfaction with your tutoring services and helping them achieve their educational goals. This includes regular check-ins, progress updates, and open communication channels that allow for feedback and adjustments.

Effective communication and support can build trust and foster positive relationships between tutors, clients, and their families. It can also help identify any challenges or concerns early on, allowing for prompt solutions and improving overall satisfaction with the tutoring experience.

To provide ongoing communication and support, tutors should establish clear communication channels with clients and their families, such as email, phone, or messaging apps. They should also schedule regular check-ins to discuss progress and address any concerns or questions. Tutors can also utilize progress reports and feedback forms to keep clients and their families informed and involved in the learning process.

Tutors should strive to be responsive and accessible, promptly addressing any questions or concerns that arise. By fostering a positive and supportive relationship with clients and their families, tutors can help them feel empowered and motivated to achieve their educational goals.

The followings are a few apps and online platforms that

could assist with providing ongoing communication and support to clients and their families:

1. Google Classroom - an online platform that allows tutors to create and manage classes, communicate with students and their families, and share assignments and resources.

2. Zoom - a video conferencing tool that enables tutors to hold virtual tutoring sessions and communicate with clients and their families in real-time.

3. Edmentum - a comprehensive online learning platform that includes instructional materials, assessments, and progress-tracking features, as well as a communication tool that allows tutors to connect with clients and their families.

4. Remind - a messaging app that enables tutors to communicate directly with clients and their families via text message without sharing personal phone numbers.

5. TutorBird - a management software that includes scheduling, invoicing, and communication tools, as well as a portal for clients and their families to access lesson materials and progress reports.

These apps and online platforms can help streamline communication and support between tutors, clients, and their families and improve overall client satisfaction and progress toward educational goals. By providing quality tutoring services, you can build a loyal client base and position your business as a leader in the field of education.

In conclusion, providing quality tutoring services is essential for any successful tutoring business. Developing a personalized learning plan for each client, utilizing a variety of teaching strategies and materials, incorporating assessments and feedback, creating a positive and supportive learning environment, and providing ongoing communication and support to clients and their families are all critical components of providing high-quality tutoring services.

Personalized learning plans consider each individual client's unique needs and preferences, creating an environment conducive to learning and growth. Utilizing a variety of teaching strategies and materials, such as visual aids, technology, and hands-on activities, can help engage clients and accommodate their learning preferences. Incorporating assessments and feedback can help identify areas for improvement, track progress, and provide positive reinforcement. Creating a positive and supportive learning environment fosters confidence and self-esteem in clients, making them more receptive to learning. Finally, providing ongoing communication and support to clients and their families helps build trust and fosters positive relationships.

There are many tools and resources available to assist tutors in providing high-quality tutoring services, such as online platforms, assessment tools, and communication apps. By incorporating these resources into their tutoring business, tutors can streamline their services, enhance the learning experience for their clients, and position themselves as leaders in the field of education. Overall, providing quality tutoring services requires a commitment to understanding and meeting the unique needs of each individual client and a dedication to ongoing improvement and growth.

Chapter Thirteen

Managing Client Relationships

Welcome to Chapter 13 of The Ultimate Guide to Starting and Growing a Successful Tutoring Business, where we will explore the critical importance of managing client relationships in your tutoring business. In the education industry, strong client relationships are not just a nice-to-have but are essential for the long-term success of your business.

As a tutor, it is not enough to simply provide quality services. You must also take a proactive approach to building and maintaining strong relationships with your clients. This involves effective communication, regular feedback, and a commitment to excellence and client satisfaction.

In this chapter, we will delve into some practical tips and strategies for managing client relationships in your tutoring business. We will explore how to establish clear expectations and goals with your clients, provide regular feedback and progress reports, encourage open and honest communication, and provide exceptional customer service. We will also discuss how developing a referral program and incentives can reward loyal clients and encourage them to refer new clients to your business.

By the end of this chapter, you will understand the critical role that strong client relationships play in the success of your tutoring business. You will have a toolbox of practical tips and strategies that you can use to build and maintain long-lasting relationships with your clients. So, let's dive in and explore the art of managing client relationships in the tutoring industry.

Building and maintaining strong client relationships is essential for the long-term success of your tutoring business. This involves effective communication, regular feedback, and a commitment to excellence and client satisfaction.

Some tips for managing client relationships in your tutoring business include:

Establish clear expectations and goals with your clients at the outset of your tutoring relationship

The success of any tutoring relationship relies heavily on communication and mutual understanding. To ensure a positive and fruitful relationship with your clients, it is important to establish clear expectations and goals from the very beginning. Why is it important to have clear expectations and establish Goals? Without clear expectations and goals, misunderstandings and unmet expectations can quickly sour a tutoring relationship. Students and their families may have certain expectations of the tutoring process that are not aligned with what you provide. Conversely, you may have goals for your students that are not communicated effectively, leading to frustration and unmet expectations on both sides. By establishing clear expectations and goals at the outset of your tutoring relationship, you can set the stage for a positive, productive, and successful experience for both you and your clients.

To establish clear expectations and goals, consider the following steps:

1. Conduct an initial consultation with the student and their family to discuss their goals and expectations for the tutoring relationship.

2. Clarify your own goals and expectations for the student based on their individual needs and your expertise as a tutor.

3. Develop a personalized tutoring plan that outlines the specific goals, objectives, and methods you will use to help the student achieve their academic goals.

4. Set clear expectations for scheduling, communication, and feedback, including any policies or procedures related to missed sessions or cancellations.

5. Review the tutoring plan and expectations with the student and their family, and ensure that everyone is on the same page before beginning the tutoring relationship.

By following these steps, you can establish clear expectations and goals for your tutoring relationship, leading to improved communication, greater satisfaction, and better student outcomes.

Providing regular feedback and progress reports to your clients and their families.

Providing regular feedback and progress reports is crucial to managing client relationships in your tutoring business. As a tutor, it's important to keep your clients and their families informed about their student's progress in their studies. Providing regular feedback and progress reports can help to build trust and confidence with your clients and show them that you are invested in their success.

Regular feedback and progress reports are essential for several reasons. First and foremost, they provide a way to track the student's progress over time and identify areas where they may need additional support. Regular feedback and progress reports can also help keep the lines of communication open with your clients and ensure that everyone is on the same page regarding the student's academic progress. By providing regular updates, you can also help alleviate any concerns or anxieties your clients may have about their student's progress.

To provide regular feedback and progress reports, it's important to establish a system for tracking student progress and communicating that progress to your clients. This could involve setting up regular check-ins or progress reports, using online tools or software to track progress and share updates, or sending regular emails or messages to keep your clients informed. Whatever method you choose, it's important to be consistent and timely with your updates to ensure that your clients feel supported and informed throughout their student's academic journey. By providing regular feedback and progress reports, you can help to build strong relationships with your clients and position your tutoring business for long-term success.

There are a variety of online tools and software programs that can be used to provide regular feedback and progress reports to clients and their families in the tutoring business. One popular tool is Google Classroom, which allows tutors to create and share assignments, quizzes, and other educational materials with their students. Google Classroom also provides a messaging system, allowing tutors to communicate with their clients and provide feedback on their progress.

Another option is Zoom, a video conferencing software tutors can use to conduct online sessions with their clients. During these sessions, tutors can provide feedback on their client's progress and discuss areas where improvement is needed. Zoom also allows tutors to share their screens, making it easier to review homework assignments and provide real-time feedback.

Tutors can also use learning management systems like Moodle or Canvas to provide progress reports and feedback to their clients and families. These platforms allow tutors to create and share course materials, track student progress, and provide regular feedback on assignments and assessments.

Overall, the online tools and software programs available for providing regular feedback and progress reports to clients and their families are numerous and varied. Tutors should choose the tools that best suit their needs and their client's needs, considering factors like ease of use, cost, and compatibility with their existing systems.

Encourage open and honest communication and actively solicit feedback and suggestions from your clients

Encouraging open and honest communication and actively soliciting your clients' feedback and suggestions is a crucial aspect of managing client relationships in your tutoring business. By encouraging open and honest communication and actively soliciting feedback and suggestions from your clients, you can gain valuable insights into their needs and expectations. This helps you to tailor your services and approach to better meet their needs and achieve their goals. It also shows your clients that you value their opinions and are committed to providing exceptional customer service.

You can encourage open and honest communication and solicit feedback and suggestions from your clients in several ways. One way is to schedule regular check-ins or progress meetings where you can discuss their progress and address any concerns they may have. You can also provide them with surveys or feedback forms to fill out anonymously, which can help them feel more comfortable sharing their thoughts and opinions. Another way is to create an open-door policy where clients feel comfortable reaching out to you at any time with their questions or concerns. Additionally, promptly responding to feedback and suggestions and taking action can help build trust and strengthen your client relationships.

Some software programs and websites that can be used for encouraging open and honest communication and actively soliciting feedback and suggestions from clients include:

1. SurveyMonkey - A website that allows you to create and send surveys to your clients and collect feedback from them.
2. Typeform - A platform for creating engaging and interactive surveys and feedback forms.
3. Google Forms - A free tool for creating surveys and feedback forms that can be easily shared with clients.
4. Slack - A team communication and collaboration platform that can be used to communicate with clients and receive feedback in real-time.
5. Trello - A project management tool that can be used to manage client feedback and suggestions.
6. Asana - A project management tool that can be used to communicate with clients, receive feedback, and track progress.
7. Zoom - A video conferencing platform that can be used for

virtual meetings and consultations with clients.

8. Skype - A popular video and voice calling platform that can be used for communicating with clients and receiving feedback.

9. WhatsApp - A messaging platform that can be used for communicating with clients and receiving feedback.

These software programs and websites can be integrated into your tutoring business to encourage open and honest communication and actively solicit feedback and suggestions from your clients.

Provide exceptional customer service and go above and beyond to meet your clients' needs and expectations

Providing exceptional customer service is a critical component of building a successful tutoring business. It involves delivering personalized service that exceeds clients' expectations and anticipates their needs. Providing exceptional customer service is essential because it sets your business apart from competitors, builds customer loyalty, and generates positive word-of-mouth referrals. It can also lead to higher customer satisfaction and retention rates, which can help grow your business and increase revenue.

There are several ways to provide exceptional customer service in your tutoring business. One way is to offer personalized attention to each client by getting to know their individual learning needs and goals. This can involve conducting an initial consultation to assess their needs and then developing a customized tutoring plan that addresses their specific challenges. Another way to provide exceptional customer service is to be responsive to clients' inquiries and concerns. This means being available to answer questions promptly, providing regular progress updates, and actively seeking feedback on how you can improve your services.

Going above and beyond to meet your clients' needs and expectations is also a key aspect of exceptional customer service. This can involve offering flexible scheduling options, providing additional resources or materials to supplement their learning, or offering incentives to reward loyal clients.

Several websites can be used to provide exceptional customer service and go above and beyond to meet clients' needs and expectations. Some examples include:

1. Help Scout: This customer service software helps businesses to communicate with their clients through multiple channels, including email, chat, and social media. It also provides collaboration tools for customer support teams.

2. Zendesk: This is another popular customer service software that provides tools for tracking customer interactions and managing support tickets. It also includes chat, phone support, and social media integration features.

3. Intercom: This software provides live chat, email, and in-app messaging tools to help businesses communicate with their clients in real-time. It also includes features such as automated messaging and targeted campaigns.

4. Freshdesk: This cloud-based customer service software provides tools for managing customer inquiries across multiple channels, including email, phone, and social media. It also includes features such as self-service portals and knowledge bases.

5. HubSpot: This all-in-one marketing and sales platform includes customer service software that provides tools for managing customer inquiries and tracking customer interactions. It also includes features such as chatbots and automated email responses.

6. Salesforce: This popular customer relationship management (CRM) software includes a customer service module that provides tools for managing customer inquiries and support tickets. It also includes features such as knowledge bases and chatbots.

7. Gorgias: This customer service software is designed specifically for e-commerce businesses and provides tools for managing customer inquiries across multiple channels, including email, chat, and social media. It also includes features such as automation and customer data integration.

Overall, providing exceptional customer service is a critical component of building and maintaining strong client relationships in your tutoring business. By delivering personalized service, being responsive to clients' needs, and going above and beyond to meet their expectations, you can position your business for long-term success.

Develop a referral program and incentives to reward loyal clients and encourage them to refer new clients to your business

Developing a referral program and incentives to reward loyal clients effectively promotes your tutoring business and attracts new clients. Referral programs are designed to encourage your existing clients to refer their friends and family members to your tutoring business, while incentives help to reward loyal clients for their continued patronage. Referral programs are a powerful marketing tool that can help your tutoring business grow and thrive. By leveraging your existing client base, you can tap into a network of potential clients who are already familiar with your services and may be more likely to trust and recommend your business to others. Incentives can further incentivize your clients to refer new clients to your business, creating a win-win situation for your business and clients.

To develop a successful referral program and incentives for

your tutoring business, you can consider offering rewards such as discounts on future tutoring sessions, gift cards, or even cash bonuses for each new client referred to your business. You can also use social media platforms and email marketing campaigns to promote your referral program and encourage your clients to share it with their friends and family members. By tracking the success of your referral program and regularly evaluating its effectiveness, you can continue to refine and optimize your program over time to ensure its ongoing success.

The following software programs and websites are some of the tools that can be used to assist with developing a referral program and incentives for your tutoring business:

1. ReferralCandy: This website allows you to create a referral program that rewards your customers for referring their friends and family to your business. It also helps you track and manage your referrals and incentives.

2. Ambassador: This software program lets you create and manage a referral program that includes rewards and incentives. It also includes analytics and reporting to help you track the success of your program.

3. TapMango: This platform lets you create a loyalty program that rewards your customers for repeat business and referrals. It also includes features for tracking customer engagement and retention.

4. Smile.io: This website lets you create a referral program that rewards customers with points for referring new customers to your business. The points can then be redeemed for discounts or other rewards.

5. Fivestars: This software program allows you to create a loyalty program that rewards customers for repeat business and referrals. It also includes features for sending targeted promotions and offers to your customers.

Building and maintaining strong client relationships can establish a positive reputation and position your tutoring business for long-term success.

In conclusion, building and maintaining strong client relationships is vital for the success of your tutoring business. Effective communication, regular feedback, and a commitment to excellence and client satisfaction are essential for establishing trust and building long-lasting relationships with your clients. By establishing clear expectations and goals at the outset of your tutoring relationship, you can set the stage for a positive, productive, and successful experience for both you and your clients. Providing regular feedback and progress reports, encouraging open and honest communication, and exceptional customer service are critical components of managing client relationships in your tutoring business. Additionally, developing a referral program and incentives to reward loyal clients and encourage them to refer new clients to your business can help you to promote your tutoring services and attract new clients. By using the online tools and software programs available for providing regular feedback, managing customer relationships, and developing referral programs, you can position your tutoring business for long-term success. By following these tips, you can build and maintain strong client relationships, establish a positive reputation, and position your tutoring business for long-term success.

Chapter Fourteen

Scaling Your Business

As a successful tutor, you have built a reputation for delivering exceptional service and achieving outstanding results for your clients. However, as your business grows, you may find yourself facing new challenges and opportunities. Perhaps you have reached the limits of what you can achieve as a solo practitioner, or you may be interested in exploring new markets or service offerings. Whatever your goals are, scaling your tutoring business can be a smart and strategic way to achieve them.

Scaling your business involves taking deliberate steps to grow and expand your operations. This may include developing a growth strategy, hiring additional staff, investing in new technologies and resources, expanding your marketing efforts, and developing new service offerings. By scaling your business, you can increase your revenue, reach new clients, and position your business for long-term success and sustainability.

In this chapter, we will explore some of the key strategies and considerations for scaling your tutoring business. Whether you are a solo practitioner looking to hire additional staff or a well-established business seeking to expand into new markets, this chapter will provide you with the guidance and insights you need to achieve your goals. So, sit back, grab a pen and paper, and let's dive into the exciting world of scaling your tutoring business.

Once you've established a successful tutoring business, you may be ready to scale your operations and expand your services. This involves developing a growth strategy, hiring additional staff, and expanding your marketing efforts to reach new markets and clients.

Some tips for scaling your tutoring business include:

Develop a growth strategy that outlines your goals and strategies for expansion

What is a growth strategy, and why is it important for scaling your tutoring business? A growth strategy is a plan that outlines the goals and strategies for expanding your business. It is important because it provides a clear roadmap for your business to achieve growth and success. Without a growth strategy, your business may struggle to expand and could even stagnate.

How do you develop a growth strategy for your tutoring business? The first step is to define your business goals. What do you want to achieve by expanding your business? Do you want to increase revenue, reach new clients, or offer new services? Once you clearly understand your goals, you can start developing strategies for achieving them.

One strategy for growth is to diversify your services.

Consider offering additional services, such as test preparation or college admissions counseling, to meet the evolving needs of your clients. Another strategy is to expand your marketing efforts to reach new markets and clients. You could target new geographic areas or demographic groups to expand your client base.

It is also important to assess your current resources and capabilities. Do you have the staff, technology, and financial resources necessary to support growth and expansion? If not, you may need to hire additional staff, invest in new technologies, or secure funding to support your growth.

Once you have developed your growth strategy, it is important to regularly monitor and evaluate your progress. This will help you to adjust as needed and ensure that your business is on track to achieve its goals.

In summary, developing a growth strategy is essential for scaling your tutoring business. By defining your goals and strategies for expansion, diversifying your services, expanding your marketing efforts, assessing your resources, and monitoring your progress, you can position your business for long-term success and sustainability.

Hire additional staff, such as tutors, administrative staff, or marketing professionals, to support your growth and expansion

Hiring additional staff is a crucial step toward scaling your tutoring business. As your business grows, you'll need more people to help you manage the workload and take on new clients. Depending on your business needs, these staff members can include tutors, administrative staff, or marketing professionals. Hiring additional staff is essential to support your growth and expansion. As you bring on more clients and expand your services, you'll need more people to help you manage the workload. This will help you avoid burnout and ensure you can provide high-quality services to your clients. Additionally, having a team of experts in different areas, such as marketing or administration, can help you streamline your operations and provide a better overall experience for your clients.

When hiring additional staff, it's important to be strategic and deliberate in your approach. First, assess your business needs and identify the areas where you need additional support. This could be in tutoring, administration, marketing, or other areas. Next, create a job description and define the qualifications you're looking for in potential candidates. Be specific about the skills, experience, and personality traits you're seeking to ensure that you find the right fit for your team.

Once you've identified potential candidates, conduct thorough interviews and ask for references to ensure they have the skills and experience needed to support your business. Finally, be sure to provide adequate training and support to ensure that your new staff members are set up for success in their roles. By hiring additional staff, you can ensure that your tutoring business has the support it needs to grow and succeed in the long term.

Various websites can be used to develop a growth strategy and hire additional staff to support business expansion. Here are a few examples:

1. Trello - a project management tool that can help track progress and assign tasks to team members.
2. Gusto - a cloud-based HR platform that can streamline payroll, benefits, and compliance.
3. LinkedIn - a professional networking website that can be used to search for and recruit new staff.
4. Upwork - a global freelance marketplace that can be used to find freelancers for various roles such as marketing or administrative support.
5. Glassdoor - a job search and company review website that can be used to research potential hires and gain insight into industry salaries and benefits.
6. Indeed - a job search website that can be used to post job openings and search for potential candidates.
7. ZipRecruiter - a job board that can be used to post job openings and reach a broad pool of job seekers.
8. Google Suite - a set of productivity tools that can be used for

collaboration, communication, and project management.

9. Zoom - a video conferencing tool that can be used for remote interviews and team meetings.

These are just a few examples of websites that can be used to achieve business growth and expansion. It's important to consider the unique needs of your business when selecting tools and resources.

Invest in new technologies and resources to enhance your services and reach new clients, such as online tutoring platforms or educational software

Investing in new technologies and resources can greatly enhance your tutoring business and help you reach new clients. Online tutoring platforms and educational software are just a couple of examples of the many ways you can use technology to improve your services and expand your reach. There are many benefits to investing in new technologies and resources for your tutoring business. For one, online tutoring platforms can allow you to offer your services to clients who may not be able to attend in-person sessions, greatly expanding your potential customer base. Additionally, educational software can help you create more engaging and interactive lessons for your students, improving their overall learning experience.

To invest in new technologies and resources for your

tutoring business, you can begin by researching the options available. Online tutoring platforms such as TutorMe and Wyzant offer a range of features and services to help you connect with new clients and manage your business. Educational software such as Smart Sparrow and Kahoot can provide you with tools to create more interactive and personalized lessons for your students.

Once you have identified the technologies and resources that will best suit your business, you can begin the process of integrating them into your operations. This may involve training staff on how to use new software or platforms or hiring additional team members with expertise in areas such as digital marketing or instructional design.

Here are some options for investing in new technologies and resources to enhance your tutoring services and reach new clients:

1. Online tutoring platforms: Consider investing in an online tutoring platform that allows you to conduct tutoring sessions remotely. Some popular online tutoring platforms include Zoom, Skype, Google Meet, and WizIQ.
2. Educational software: A wide range of educational software available can help enhance your tutoring services. Some popular options include Quizlet, Khan Academy, Duolingo, and Edmentum.
3. Learning management systems: A learning management

system (LMS) can help you manage your tutoring business, track student progress, and provide a centralized location for educational resources. Some popular LMS options include Canvas, Moodle, and Blackboard.

4. Video content creation tools: Consider investing in video content creation tools to create educational videos to share with your students. Some popular options include Camtasia, Animoto, and Powtoon.

5. Learning games and apps: Gamifying learning can effectively engage students and enhance the learning experience. Consider investing in learning games and apps, such as Kahoot!, BrainPOP, and Prodigy.

Investing in new technologies and resources can be a key component of scaling your tutoring business and ensuring its long-term success. By staying up-to-date with your field's latest tools and trends, you can continue to provide high-quality services to your clients and grow your business over time.

Expand your marketing efforts to reach new markets and clients, such as targeting new geographic areas or demographic groups

Expanding your marketing efforts is a crucial step in scaling your tutoring business. By targeting new geographic areas or demographic groups, you can reach new clients and expand your business's reach. Expanding your marketing efforts helps your tutoring business stay competitive and relevant in an ever-changing marketplace. It allows you to connect with new clients, grow your revenue, and establish your business as a leader in the industry.

There are several ways to expand your marketing efforts and reach new markets and clients. One effective strategy is to develop targeted marketing campaigns that speak directly to the needs and interests of your desired audience. This can include creating customized messaging, developing social media campaigns, or partnering with local organizations or schools to promote your services. You can also consider attending education conferences or events to network with potential clients and establish your business as a thought leader in the industry. Another option is to invest in digital marketing efforts, such as search engine optimization (SEO) or pay-per-click (PPC) advertising. By optimizing your website for search engines or running targeted ads, you can attract new clients who are actively searching for tutoring services.

Here are some options to expand your marketing efforts and reach new markets and clients:

1. **Utilize social media platforms:** Social media platforms such as Facebook, Instagram, and Twitter can be powerful tools to reach a wider audience. By creating engaging content and targeted ads, you can attract potential clients and

build your brand.

2. **Attend education fairs and events:** Participating in education fairs and events can help you reach potential clients and showcase your tutoring services. You can network with other professionals in the industry and gather valuable insights on the latest trends and demands.

3. **Offer referral incentives:** Encourage your existing clients to refer their friends and family by offering referral incentives such as discounts or free sessions. Word of mouth is a powerful marketing tool and can help you expand your client base.

4. **Collaborate with schools and universities:** Partnering with local schools and universities can help you tap into a new demographic and gain access to potential clients. You can offer your services as an after-school program or provide test preparation services for college-bound students.

5. **Use targeted advertising:** Utilize online advertising platforms such as Google AdWords or Facebook Ads to target specific geographic areas or demographic groups. This can help you reach potential clients who are actively searching for tutoring services in their area.

6. **Build a strong online presence:** Ensure your website is optimized for search engines and your online profiles are complete and up-to-date. This can help you attract potential

clients who are searching for tutoring services online.

7. **Offer free trial sessions:** Offering free trial sessions can help potential clients get a taste of your services and build trust in your brand. This can lead to new clients and repeat business.

Expanding your marketing efforts requires a strategic approach and a willingness to experiment with new tactics and channels. By continually refining your marketing strategies, you can effectively reach new markets and clients and position your tutoring business for long-term success.

Develop new service offerings, such as test preparation or college admissions counseling, to meet the evolving needs of your clients

Developing new service offerings is an effective way to meet clients' changing needs in the tutoring industry. As the education landscape evolves, students may require additional support and resources to achieve their academic goals. By offering new services such as test preparation or college admissions counseling, tutoring businesses can provide valuable solutions that meet the unique needs of their clients. There are several benefits to developing new service offerings for a tutoring business. Firstly, it can help to differentiate your business from competitors and establish your brand as a leader in the industry. Secondly, it can create new revenue streams and increase profitability by attracting new clients and expanding existing relationships. Finally, it can help to enhance client satisfaction and retention by offering a comprehensive suite of services that address their needs at every stage of their academic journey.

Developing new service offerings requires a thoughtful and strategic approach. It begins by understanding the needs and preferences of your clients and identifying areas where you can provide additional value. Once you have identified these areas, you can begin to develop a plan for new service offerings that align with your business goals and meet your clients' needs. This may involve hiring additional staff with specialized skills or expertise, investing in new technologies or resources, or partnering with other organizations to provide complementary services. By taking a proactive approach to developing new service offerings, tutoring businesses can stay ahead of the curve and position themselves for long-term success.

The following are some options for developing new service offerings in a tutoring business:

1. Test preparation services for standardized tests such as SAT, ACT, GRE, GMAT, LSAT, and MCAT.
2. College admissions counseling services help students navigate the application process, prepare for interviews, and

write strong personal statements.

3. Specialized tutoring services for students with learning disabilities or language barriers.

4. Advanced Placement (AP) exam preparation services.

5. Summer tutoring camps or intensive tutoring programs.

6. Online tutoring services provide flexibility and convenience for students.

7. Professional development workshops for educators and tutors to improve their teaching skills and techniques.

8. Tutoring services for adult learners, such as language instruction or workforce development.

9. Career counseling and coaching services to help students explore their interests and identify potential career paths.

10. Enrichment programs in subjects such as creative writing, STEM (science, technology, engineering, and math), or the arts.

In conclusion, scaling your tutoring business is an important step toward achieving long-term success and sustainability. It involves developing a growth strategy, hiring additional staff, investing in new technologies and resources, expanding your marketing efforts, and developing new service offerings. By taking a strategic and deliberate approach to scaling your business, you can differentiate your brand, expand your client base, and provide valuable solutions that meet the evolving needs of your clients. As you continue to grow and evolve, it's important to regularly monitor and evaluate your progress, making adjustments as needed to ensure that you're on track to achieve your goals. By following these tips and strategies, you can position your tutoring business for success in a competitive and dynamic marketplace.

Chapter Fifteen

Overcoming Challenges and Staying Competitive

As a tutor, you know that building and growing a successful tutoring business is no small feat. Economic downturns, increased competition, and changes in the education industry can all impact your business and require you to constantly adapt and innovate to stay competitive. But how can you navigate these challenges and stay ahead of the curve? This chapter will explore some tips and strategies for overcoming challenges and staying competitive in the tutoring industry. From staying up-to-date with changes in the education industry to fostering a positive work environment and building a strong reputation, we'll cover everything you need to know to position your tutoring business for long-term success and growth. So if you're ready to take your tutoring business to the next level, let's get started!

Building and growing a successful tutoring business is a rewarding endeavor that can significantly impact students' lives. However, it is not without its challenges. Economic downturns, for example, can cause families to cut back on discretionary spending, making it more difficult to attract and retain clients. Similarly, increased competition in the tutoring industry can make it harder to stand out from the crowd and win new business.

Changes in the education industry can also have a significant impact on tutoring businesses. As technology advances, online tutoring services are becoming increasingly popular, making it essential to keep up with the latest trends and offerings to remain competitive. Additionally, changes in curriculum and teaching methods can impact the demand for certain types of tutoring services, requiring businesses to adapt and innovate to meet the evolving needs of students and parents.

In order to overcome these challenges and succeed in the tutoring industry, businesses must be prepared to adapt and innovate. This may involve investing in new technologies, developing new service offerings, and continuously improving the skills and knowledge of staff. By staying ahead of the curve and delivering exceptional service, tutoring businesses can stand out from the competition and position themselves for long-term success and growth.

In the following section, we will explore several tips for overcoming challenges and staying competitive in the tutoring industry:

Stay up-to-date with changes in the education industry and adapt your services and offerings to meet evolving needs and trends

The education industry is constantly changing in today's

fast-paced and ever-evolving world. From advancements in technology to new teaching methodologies, these changes can have a significant impact on the tutoring industry. As a result, it's crucial for tutoring businesses to stay up-to-date with the latest trends and needs to remain relevant and competitive.

Adapting your tutoring services and offerings to meet evolving needs and trends is crucial for the success of your business. By staying current with the latest changes in the education industry, you can better understand the needs of your clients and offer relevant and effective services that meet their requirements. This ensures your client's satisfaction and positions your business as a leader in the industry.

There are several ways to stay up-to-date with changes in the education industry and adapt your services and offerings accordingly. One effective approach is to continuously invest in professional development and training. By doing so, you and your staff can acquire the latest knowledge and skills in the field of education and apply them to your tutoring services.

Another way is to conduct market research and gather client feedback to identify their changing needs and preferences. This can help you tailor your services and offerings to better meet their requirements and stand out from the competition.

Lastly, networking and staying connected with other

professionals in the education industry can provide valuable insights into emerging trends and changes. Attending conferences, participating in industry associations, and collaborating with other businesses can help you stay current and relevant in the industry.

The following are some options for staying up-to-date with changes in the education industry and adapting your tutoring services and offerings:

1. **Attend conferences and seminars:** Attending conferences and seminars can provide valuable insights into emerging trends, changes in the industry, and new teaching techniques. It can also be an excellent opportunity to network with other professionals in the field.

2. **Follow industry publications:** Reading education publications and journals can keep you informed about the latest news, research, and developments in the field. It can also help you stay ahead of the competition by adopting new teaching methodologies and strategies. Some examples of publications related to staying up-to-date with changes in the education industry and adapting services to meet evolving needs and trends are EdTech Magazine, Education Week, ASCD (Association for Supervision and Curriculum Development) SmartBrief, TeachThought, and EdSurge.

3. **Engage in ongoing training and professional development:** Continuously investing in training and

development can help you stay current with the latest teaching methodologies and technologies. It can also help you develop new skills and approaches to enhance your services and attract new clients.

4. **Collaborate with other professionals:** Collaborating with other professionals, such as teachers, school administrators, and other tutors, can help you stay informed about changes in the education industry. It can also provide opportunities to share knowledge, insights, and best practices.

5. **Conduct regular research and analysis:** Conducting regular research and analysis can help you identify emerging trends and changes in the education industry. It can also help you understand your client's needs and preferences, allowing you to tailor your services to meet their evolving needs.

6. **Solicit feedback from clients:** Soliciting feedback from your clients can help you understand their needs and preferences. It can also provide valuable insights into areas where you may need to improve your services or adapt your offerings to meet their evolving needs.

7. **Utilize technology:** Utilizing technology, such as online tutoring platforms and educational apps, can help you stay up-to-date with educational industry changes. It can also provide opportunities to deliver your services more efficiently and effectively.

By staying up-to-date with changes in the education industry and adapting your tutoring services and offerings, you can position your business for success and growth in the highly competitive and dynamic field of education.

Continuously invest in professional development and training to ensure that you and your staff have the latest knowledge and skills in the field of education

Investing in professional development and training for you and your staff is an essential aspect of building and growing a successful tutoring business. By committing to continuous learning and improvement, you can ensure that you provide the best possible service to your clients and stay competitive in the ever-evolving field of education.

In today's fast-paced and dynamic world, staying up-to-date with the latest trends, techniques, and technologies in education is crucial. By investing in professional development, you can stay ahead of the curve and provide your clients with the most effective and innovative solutions to their educational needs. Additionally, ongoing training and learning opportunities can help you and your staff feel more engaged, motivated, and fulfilled in your work, leading to better job satisfaction and retention.

There are many ways to invest in professional development and training, including attending conferences and workshops, taking online courses and certifications, joining professional organizations, and working with mentors and coaches. It's essential to create a culture of learning and growth within your organization, where staff members are encouraged and supported in their professional development endeavors. You can attract top talent and retain valuable staff members by providing ongoing training and development opportunities, leading to a more successful and sustainable tutoring business.

Develop a culture of innovation and creativity, and actively seek out new ideas and approaches to enhance your services and differentiate your business from the competition

Developing a culture of innovation and creativity is crucial for any business to stay competitive and succeed in the long run. This is especially true in the tutoring industry, where adapting and differentiating your services from the competition is always necessary. Innovation and creativity are essential because they allow you to offer unique services that stand out from the competition. It can also help you anticipate your client's needs and expectations and proactively offer new solutions and ideas.

To develop a culture of innovation and creativity in your tutoring business, you must encourage your staff to think outside the box and develop new ideas. This can be done by setting up regular brainstorming sessions, where everyone is encouraged to share their thoughts and ideas. You should also actively seek out new approaches and ideas from other industries and experts and adapt them to your tutoring business. This could involve attending industry conferences, networking events, or online forums to learn about new trends and ideas.

It's also essential to foster a supportive and collaborative work environment where everyone feels comfortable sharing their thoughts and ideas. By promoting a culture of innovation and creativity, you can stay ahead of the curve and offer innovative services that meet the evolving needs of your clients.

Foster a positive and supportive work environment that encourages excellence and collaboration among your staff and fosters strong relationships with your clients

Foster a positive and supportive work environment that encourages excellence and collaboration among your staff and fosters strong relationships with your clients. Creating a positive work environment is essential to the success of any tutoring business. A supportive and collaborative workplace can boost staff morale and increase productivity, leading to better outcomes for clients. Building strong relationships with clients is key to retaining business and fostering loyalty.

Create a culture of open communication where internal

stakeholders are encouraged to engage in open communication with one another to foster a supportive environment where everyone feels comfortable sharing ideas, expressing concerns, and giving and receiving feedback. Offer professional development opportunities by providing opportunities for staff to learn and grow in their roles. This can include attending conferences, workshops, or online courses, as well as offering in-house training and mentoring programs.

Recognize and reward excellence by celebrating staff members who go above and beyond in their roles. This can include acknowledging achievements publicly, offering bonuses or incentives, or providing opportunities for career advancement. Encourage teamwork and collaboration in order to foster a spirit of collaboration among staff members by encouraging teamwork on projects and initiatives. This can include regular team-building activities or events, as well as providing opportunities for staff to work together on projects or initiatives.

Prioritize client satisfaction by fostering strong relationships by providing exceptional customer service, being responsive to their needs and concerns, and going above and beyond to ensure their satisfaction. This can include regular check-ins, personalized tutoring plans, and offering additional resources or support as needed.

Build a strong reputation and brand identity through exceptional customer service, effective marketing, and a commitment to excellence and client satisfaction

Building a strong reputation and brand identity through exceptional customer service, effective marketing, and a commitment to excellence and client satisfaction is key to the success of any tutoring business. A strong reputation and brand identity can differentiate your business from competitors, increase client loyalty and retention, and ultimately lead to growth and profitability. Exceptional customer service means going above and beyond to meet the needs of your clients, whether it's providing personalized learning plans or responding quickly and effectively to any issues or concerns. Effective marketing involves identifying your target audience, crafting a clear and compelling message, and utilizing a mix of traditional and digital marketing channels to reach potential clients. Finally, a commitment to excellence and client satisfaction means consistently delivering high-quality services and ensuring your clients feel valued and supported at every step. By building a strong reputation and brand identity, your tutoring business can establish itself as a trusted and respected leader in the education industry.

In conclusion, starting and growing a successful tutoring business is an achievable goal for anyone with a passion for education and a drive to succeed. The Ultimate Guide to Starting and Growing a Successful Tutoring Business has provided a comprehensive roadmap for aspiring entrepreneurs, offering practical advice on every aspect of building and scaling a tutoring business. From identifying your target market and developing your niche to creating a solid business plan, developing a marketing strategy, and managing client relationships, this guide has covered all the necessary steps to launch and grow a successful tutoring business.

But the journey doesn't end there. As your business expands, you will face new challenges and competition, which is why it's crucial to continuously adapt, innovate, and stay up-to-date with the latest trends and best practices in the industry. Following the strategies outlined in this guide and keeping an open mind to new ideas and approaches can position your business for long-term success and growth.

Remember, success in the tutoring industry is not just about profits and financial gains. It's about making a positive impact on the lives of your clients, fostering a love for learning, and helping students achieve their full potential. With the right mindset, dedication, and guidance, you can turn your passion for education into a thriving tutoring business and make a difference in the world.

About the Author

Maurice C. Hill is a man of many talents and experiences, including that of a former Adjunct Professor at Mercer University and a decorated Sailor who served in the United States Navy during the first Gulf War. Maurice's dedication to his country and service in the Navy instilled in him the values of discipline, teamwork, and commitment, which he continues to uphold in his personal and professional life.

After completing his military service, Maurice began his academic journey by earning undergraduate degrees in Business Administration and Education from Georgia State University. He later earned a Bachelor's degree in Business Management and a Master's degree in Business Administration from the University of Phoenix. Maurice's passion for counseling individuals and families led him to pursue a Master's degree in Clinical Mental Health Counseling from Mercer University, where he also studied Counselor Education and Supervision while in a Ph.D. program.

Maurice's vast knowledge and experience in various fields have made him a sought-after authority in his respective areas. He is currently a licensed real estate broker and a licensed professional counselor (LPC) in the state of Georgia, a National Certified Counselor (NCC), a member of the Dekalb Board of Realtors, the Georgia Association of Realtors, and the National Association of

Realtors. Maurice began his real estate career in 1997 and later became the chief executive officer (CEO) and qualifying broker of All Properties Professionals Realty in East Point, Georgia. He also serves as the founder and CEO of One United Publishing, where he helps business owners achieve their goals and aspirations through self-help books.

Maurice's dedication to helping others extends beyond his professional life. While in graduate school with a focus on training master's level clinical mental health counselors, Maurice became concerned about helping budding entrepreneurs who desire to own and operate their businesses. Inspired by the strong desire and sense of urgency related to helping business owners, Maurice decided to apply for and eventually enroll in the Harvard University entrepreneurship program. With his combined education and experience as an educator, business owner, and counselor, Maurice decided to write a group of self-help books.

Maurice has lectured nationally and internationally on various topics related to mental health counseling, including Vicarious Trauma, the Psychological Aspects of Multiculturalism in Counseling, and Trauma-Focused Cognitive Behavioral Therapy. He has been honored with numerous awards throughout his career, including The Empire Board of Realtist Million Dollar Club Award from 2000-2006 and the Dekalb Board of Realtors Pinnacle Award in 2020, 2021, and 2022. He is also a member of the Chi Sigma Iota

International Honor Society.

In addition to his professional accomplishments, Maurice is an avid traveler who has visited nearly 30 countries. His experiences abroad have enriched his understanding of humanity and the natural world. Studying the diverse cultures, histories, and socio-political landscapes of the places he has visited have deepened his love for humanity and nature. These experiences have opened his eyes to the complexity and beauty of our world and have inspired him to be a lifelong learner and advocate for positive change.

Maurice C. Hill is a remarkable individual who has impacted the lives of many through his passion, dedication, and expertise. His unwavering commitment to helping people achieve their goals and aspirations inspires others. With extensive knowledge and experience in multiple fields, Maurice is highly regarded as an authority and sought-after speaker. Additionally, Maurice has pursued his passion for flying airplanes by training at the Aviation Career Enrichment Inc in Atlanta, Georgia. His love for adventure and exploration, coupled with his dedication to his work, make him an inspiration to all. When he's not up in the air, Maurice enjoys spending quality time with his family.

www.ingramcontent.com/pod-product-compliance
Lightning Source LLC
Chambersburg PA
CBHW040543160726

48196CB00086B/592